JOHN McCAIN
AN AMERICAN HERO

JOHN McCAIN

AN AMERICAN HERO

By Beatrice Gormley

ALADDIN

New York London Toronto Sydney New Delhi

ALADDIN

An imprint of Simon & Schuster Children's Publishing Division

1230 Avenue of the Americas, New York, New York 10020

First Aladdin hardcover edition October 2018

Text copyright © 2018 by Beatrice Gormley

Official Senate portrait by Frank A. Fey

Also available in an Aladdin paperback edition.

For information about special discounts for bulk purchases,
please contact Simon & Schuster Special Sales at 1-866-506-1949
or business@simonandschuster.com.

The Simon & Schuster Speakers Bureau can bring authors to your
live event. For more information or to book an event contact the
Simon & Schuster Speakers Bureau at 1-866-248-3049
or visit our website at www.simonspeakers.com.

Jacket designed by Tiara Iandiorio

Interior designed by Mike Rosamilia

The text of this book was set in Cochin LT Std.

Manufactured in the United States of America 0918 FFG

10 9 8 7 6 5 4 3 2 1

Library of Congress Control Number 2018952389

ISBN 978-1-5344-4386-0 (hc)

ISBN 978-1-5344-4385-3 (pbk)

ISBN 978-1-5344-4387-7 (eBook)

To my husband, Bob

Contents

1. A Proud Tradition. 1

2. Johnny the Punk 11

3. Midshipman McCain 19

4. Naval Aviator 31

5. Prisoner in the Hanoi Hilton 43

6. Moving On 60

7. Big Changes 73

8. Senator McCain 84

9. An Old War and a New War 99

10. Maverick 107

11. Straight Talk 118

12. "The Dirtiest Campaign" 132

13. Defeat with Honor 149

14. Statesman McCain 167

15. The Restless Wave 182

Time Line 197

Sources 203

Chapter 1

A Proud Tradition

John Sidney McCain III, known as Johnny, was a navy kid from day one. He was born on August 29, 1936, to Roberta and John Sidney McCain Jr., in the hospital at Coco Solo Naval Air Station in the Panama Canal Zone. Johnny's father, called Jack, was assigned to a submarine stationed at Coco Solo. His grandfather, John Sidney McCain Sr. was the base commander there.

Base Commander McCain, nicknamed "Slew," doted on his new grandson. A photo of Johnny and his father and grandfather at Johnny's christening shows Jack looking serious. But Johnny's grandfather is grinning from ear to ear as he cradles his tiny grandson in his arms.

Commander McCain was even glad to babysit

Johnny. One night, going out to a party, Roberta McCain instructed her father-in-law to let the baby cry in his crib. Returning home, she was shocked to discover that Grandfather McCain had instead taken little Johnny to bed with him. "Dammit, Roberta," he tried to explain himself, "that boy has the stamp of nobility on his brow."

Johnny's parents weren't so sure, especially as Johnny became a toddler. He had fits of temper, often becoming so angry that he held his breath until he fainted. His parents were worried, but the family doctor advised them to dunk the little boy in a tub of cold water each time a tantrum began. This treatment seemed to cure Johnny's temper fits.

A few months after Johnny's birth, his family— his father, his mother, and his older sister, Jean (called Sandy)—moved to New London, Connecticut. Jack McCain had been assigned to the submarine command headquarters there. This would be only the first of Johnny McCain's many moves with his family as they followed Jack to various naval posts around the country. In 1939 the McCains moved to San Diego, California, where Jack had been appointed commander of the Naval Air Station. Only two years later, in April 1941, they were back in New London.

One Sunday toward the end of that year, five-year-old Johnny and his family happened to be standing in their front yard. A naval officer pulled his car up in front of the McCains' house and shouted to Johnny's father. "Jack! The Japanese have bombed Pearl Harbor!" It was December 7, 1941.

Jack McCain left immediately for the base. The next day President Franklin D. Roosevelt asked Congress to declare war on Japan. Soon afterward, Nazi Germany declared war on the United States. The United States entered World War II, and Johnny hardly saw his father during the next four years.

Fortunately, Roberta McCain was perfectly capable of running the family, which now included Johnny's brother, Joseph, born in 1942, by herself. A lively, enthusiastic woman, Roberta loved navy life. She was always interested in new places and experiences, and she made new friends easily.

Roberta had grown up in California as the daughter of wealthy oilman Archibald Wright and his wife, Myrtle. But she didn't mind making do on her husband's small salary as a naval officer, and she treated their frequent moves as chances for adventure. In fact, her marriage to Jack McCain had begun as an adventure, when at the age of twenty she'd married him against her family's wishes, eloping with him to Tijuana, Mexico.

Although Johnny seldom saw his father or grandfather during the war years, they were important figures in his life. Sometimes his mother would wake him up in the middle of the night to see his grandfather, stopping by on his way to his next assignment. Johnny was always delighted to see Grandfather McCain, a lively, fun-loving man. The two had had a special bond ever since Johnny was a baby in Panama, when the tough, chain-smoking naval commander babysat for him.

Johnny McCain learned as a young boy that a career in the navy was the best life—the only possible life—for a McCain man. His grandfather, who grew up on a plantation in Carroll County, Mississippi, had graduated from the United States Naval Academy at Annapolis, Maryland, in 1906. Slew McCain began serving in the navy when Theodore Roosevelt was president.

President Theodore Roosevelt had done a great deal to build up the United States Navy, and the McCains considered him one of the greatest presidents ever. To demonstrate US naval power to the world, Roosevelt sent the "Great White Fleet," a parade of battleships seven miles long, around the globe. When the fleet returned in triumph in late 1908, young Ensign McCain stood at attention on the deck of the flagship, the USS *Connecticut*, to salute President Roosevelt.

Slew McCain, short and slight, did not fit the image most people have of a military hero. But he made up for his small size with a fierce fighting spirit and unflinching courage, and his men were devoted to him. He rose to the rank of vice admiral during World War II. In the famous battle of Guadalcanal, Johnny's grandfather commanded the land-based air operations of the United States and its allies in the South Pacific. In the last year of the war, Slew McCain commanded Task Force 38 of the Third Fleet, a carrier task force that took the combat all the way from the Philippines to Japan.

Meanwhile, his son, John McCain Jr., idolized his father and yearned to be just like him. Jack McCain, also a small, slight man, graduated from the Naval Academy in 1931. He fought in World War II as commander of the submarine USS *Gunnel*, first in the Atlantic Ocean and then in the Pacific. After the war, Johnny listened to his father's thrilling stories of many narrow escapes.

Jack McCain's worst ordeal took place in the

East China Sea, as the *Gunnel* was being hunted down by three Japanese destroyers. The *Gunnel* managed to torpedo and sink one of the destroyers, but the remaining two attacked the submarine with depth charges. Commander McCain took his submarine down to three hundred feet, out of reach. After eighteen hours underwater, the carbon dioxide level of the air rose dangerously. The crew nearly suffocated, but Jack McCain managed to bring his ship and men through safely.

On September 2, 1945, the Japanese formally surrendered to the United States and its allies. Vice Admiral McCain had the honor of being one of the officers present at the ceremony on board the USS *Missouri* in Tokyo Bay. Jack McCain was also in Tokyo Bay, now commanding a captured Japanese submarine, and the father and son met for a private talk after the ceremonies. Vice Admiral McCain was extremely thin, having worn himself out in the stressful last months of the war, but he was in high spirits. It was a privilege, he told his son, to die for your principles and country.

Four days later, in the middle of a welcome-home party in Coronado, California, Johnny's grandfather dropped dead from a heart attack. He was buried with full honors in Arlington National Cemetery, the historic military cemetery outside Washington, DC, and President Harry S. Truman sent condolences to Johnny's grandmother. Soon after his death, Congress honored John S. McCain Sr. with the rank of full admiral.

After the war, Jack McCain continued to devote himself to his career in the navy. During these years he worked at the Pentagon, in Washington, DC, and the McCains had a house on Capitol Hill. Jack McCain was happiest when he was working. Even on Christmas Day, after Sandy, Johnny, and Joe had opened their presents, he'd put on his uniform and leave for the office.

As a young boy, Johnny wished his father would spend more time with him. Still, he understood, from his mother as well as his father, that it was an honor to have a father who served such a noble cause. A navy officer's family, by supporting him and his work, also shared in that proud tradition of serving and sacrificing for one's country.

Johnny also learned, as a boy, to respect the officer's code of honor. An officer did not lie, steal, or cheat. An officer kept his word. An officer knew his duty and did it, no matter how difficult. An officer accepted responsibility for his men and took care of them.

Johnny could see for himself how serious his father was about the code. His brother, Joe, commented in later life that he'd never heard his father tell a lie. Once, Roberta teasingly accused her husband of lying during a card game. He was very disturbed that she would suggest such a thing, even as a joke.

Roberta McCain set an example for her children by wholeheartedly supporting her husband's career. Beautiful and charming, she filled the social role that hardworking Jack McCain ignored. She knew that wherever they happened to move, there would be other navy families to welcome them and to look out for one another when the husbands were away.

But Roberta worried about her children's education. They moved so often that the McCain children might be either behind or ahead of the curriculum in each new school. Worse, the schools at navy bases were almost always substandard. Classes might be held in an old hangar. Teachers came and went, and sometimes no teacher at all showed up.

None of this bothered Johnny very much, because to him school was mainly a place to make friends. Like his father and grandfather, he was small for his age, but athletic and tough. He often got into a fight during his first days at a new school, just to show that he couldn't be pushed around. He was a natural leader among the children, and a favorite among adults for his good manners and cheerful temperament. In each new home, Johnny proudly showed his friends a photo of the Japanese surrender on the *Missouri*, with his grandfather in the ranks of the American officers.

To make up for the inferior navy base schools, Roberta McCain used the family's trips across the country to educate the children herself. On their way to new homes she took Johnny, Sandy, and Joe to national parks such as Carlsbad Caverns and the Grand Canyon. She planned the route so as to visit art museums, historical sites, and beautiful old churches.

When Roberta was a child in Southern California, her father had taken her and her twin sister, Rowena, on similar long road trips. Young Roberta and Rowena had learned geography, natural history, and other subjects by actually seeing the source of the Mississippi River, marveling at the Hoover Dam, and exploring Yellowstone National Park. Now Roberta wanted to give her own children the same opportunities.

When Johnny was twelve, the family had to move yet again, from Washington, DC, to Coronado, California. On this cross-country trip, Johnny and

Sandy squabbled endlessly in the backseat. Their mother ordered them to stop fighting, but Johnny answered her with a smart remark.

Finally out of patience, Roberta McCain grabbed a banana as she drove and threw it over her shoulder at Johnny. The banana hit Sandy instead, which made Johnny laugh. Really angry now, Roberta grabbed an aluminum thermos and threw it at Johnny. He wasn't hurt (aluminum is light), but he was indignant, especially when she laughed at him.

Johnny's mother, writing a letter to his father that night, reported that his namesake had become "a real pain in the neck." Up to that time, he'd been polite and cooperative, at least with adults. It was the first sign (aside from his two-year-old tantrums) of the rebellious, defiant streak for which he would become famous.

Chapter 2

Johnny the Punk

Johnny McCain grew up knowing that he would attend the US Naval Academy. His mother, his father, and everyone else in the family had always assumed that Johnny was destined for a career as a naval officer. They never thought of discussing the matter; they all just took it for granted. When it was time for college, Johnny would follow his father and grandfather to Annapolis.

Johnny wasn't particularly worried about whether he'd be able to pass the academy's entrance exams. But his parents knew the sub-standard military base schools weren't preparing him well, and they were concerned. In 1946, when Jack McCain was working in public relations for the navy in Washington, DC, the family lived in nearby Virginia. They took the chance to enroll

Johnny at St. Stephen's School, a private day school in Alexandria, Virginia.

Just before he entered St. Stephen's in the fall of 1946, Johnny spent a memorable summer with his widowed grandmother, Katherine Vaulx McCain, in Coronado, California. He stayed in a room stuffed with his father's boyhood books, and all summer he read. Johnny was impatient and restless by nature, but a good book could keep him spellbound for hours. Like his father, Johnny was thrilled with stories of high adventure by James Fenimore Cooper, Mark Twain, Rudyard Kipling, and Robert Louis Stevenson.

Johnny's father was devoted to his work and gave long hours to it. But when he was home, he made important contributions to his son's education. Jack McCain was an avid reader of history, poetry, classic novels, and biographies. He could recite long passages of poetry by heart. One of Stevenson's poems, "Requiem," was a favorite of Jack McCain's, and it became one of Johnny's as well.

At age twelve, Johnny stumbled upon a book that held a special fascination for him. He wasn't even looking for a book to read at the time. He'd just found two four-leaf clovers, supposedly good-luck charms, and he ran inside to his father's study and pulled a book off the shelf to press the clovers. That book happened to be *For Whom the Bell Tolls*, by Ernest Hemingway.

Forgetting about his four-leaf clovers, Johnny sat down and read the whole book. It was a novel about an American, Robert Jordan, who goes to Spain to help fight in the Spanish Civil War of 1936–1939. Johnny was captivated by Hemingway's story of idealism and sacrifice. In years to come, he would read *For Whom the Bell Tolls* again and again, gaining a deeper understanding each time.

After Johnny had attended St. Stephen's for three years, the McCains moved to the West Coast once more to follow Jack's career in the submarine service. Finally, in 1951, Jack and Roberta McCain felt it was time for their older son to buckle down and study harder. They decided to send him to Episcopal High School, a boys' boarding school in Alexandria, Virginia, for his tenth through twelfth years of high school.

The Episcopal High School campus, in the hills across the Potomac from Washington, looked down on the Capitol and the Washington Monument. EHS was an institution of deep traditions, founded in 1839 as the first high school in Virginia. One of the many traditions at Episcopal High School was hazing first-year students, called "rats." A "rat" was expected to address other students as "gentlemen."

Episcopal High School took pride in educating young Southern gentlemen, and most of the other boys at EHS really did come from genteel Southern families. Johnny McCain's ancestors had come from Mississippi, but he himself had grown up on navy bases around the country. He didn't even talk with a Southern accent. Furthermore, he didn't have the humble attitude expected of a new boy. By the end of his first year at EHS, he had earned the title of "Worst Rat."

Johnny McCain did not strive to fit the EHS image. In fact, he defied the image. He wore the required coat and tie, but with unwashed jeans. His school nickname was "Punk," and his yearbook picture showed him in a trench coat, smoking a cigarette. He enjoyed his reputation as a rebel.

During the spring semester of Johnny's first year at EHS, the movie *Viva Zapata!*, starring Marlon Brando, came out. Johnny's imagination was caught by this story of the noble but doomed Mexican rebel Emiliano Zapata of the early 1900s. He liked to think of himself as a brave rebel like Zapata, fighting injustice to the death.

In spite of his rebel pose, Johnny joined the EHS wrestling team and did well. The wrestling coach, Riley Deeble, was impressed with his courage. Johnny was still small for his age, but tougher than ever, going right after his opponent even if the other boy was stronger or better trained. Johnny's toughness came out in the dormitory as well as on the wrestling mat, earning him a second nickname, "McNasty," for his eagerness to fight.

However, Johnny made some good friends, such as Rives Richey, at EHS. He might have been a rebel, but he wasn't a lone rebel; he was always happiest in a group. He and a small band of friends, including Richey, got a reputation for breaking the school rules. Their favorite exploit was sneaking off campus at night to go to a movie or to explore Washington, DC.

In his classes, Johnny didn't bother to work unless he was interested in the subject. Since he was interested in English and history, his grades in those subjects were fairly good. But he was not interested in science or math, and often he barely passed those classes.

His English teacher at EHS, William B. Ravenel, gave Johnny an extra reason to work harder in his English classes. All the boys admired Mr. Ravenel, so much so that Johnny's class dedicated its yearbook to him. Mr. Ravenel had been a football star in college, and he was a decorated veteran of General George S. Patton's tank corps in World War II. He loved English literature and knew how to help his students appreciate Shakespeare's plays and other great works.

Johnny also continued to read eagerly on his own. When he was fourteen, his younger brother, Joe, saw him reading *Napoleon*, by Emil Ludwig, a biography of the brilliant general. Joe admired his brother and wanted to read the book too. But it was several hundred pages long, and Joe just couldn't finish it. Besides being several years younger, Joe wasn't as fascinated by military history as Johnny was.

In the fall semester of 1952, Johnny's second year at Episcopal High School, Dwight D. Eisenhower was elected president of the United States. Eisenhower, like Mr. Ravenel and Johnny's father and grandfather, was a veteran of World War II. General Eisenhower had been supreme commander of the Allied forces in Europe during that war, and Americans trusted him to resolve the conflict in Korea.

The Korean War had begun in 1950, when Communist North Korea invaded and nearly conquered South Korea, an ally of the United States. North

Korea was backed by Communist China, and there was a great fear in the West, especially in the United States, that Communism might overrun the world. President Truman had sent US troops to protect South Korea and stop the spread of Communism.

During much of the Korean War, Johnny's father was away from home on active duty. It was especially helpful for teenage Johnny that Mr. Ravenel, a man he admired so much, took an interest in him. Unexpectedly, Johnny's bad behavior gave him extra chances to talk with his admired teacher.

At Episcopal High School, Johnny was continually racking up demerits for breaking the rules. He then had to work off his demerits, which was usually done by walking—one mile for each demerit, around and around the circle drive in front of the school. Luckily for Johnny, another way to work off demerits was by doing chores for a teacher, and he was often assigned to yard work at Mr. Ravenel's home. Mr. Ravenel let him know that he thought Johnny had potential for leadership. No one else at the school did, but Mr. Ravenel's confidence in him made a deep impression on Johnny.

Hardly anyone at Episcopal High School even knew that Johnny intended to apply to the Naval

Academy. Rives Richey was one of Johnny's closest friends, but he was surprised when Johnny told him so during their senior year. The Naval Academy was famous for its strict discipline and difficult academic program, and its students were expected to become dedicated leaders in the military. Richey—in spite of his fondness for Punk McCain—thought his rule-breaking buddy was one of the least likely to succeed in their class.

In Johnny's mind, on the other hand, a career in the navy was the only possible choice for him. Before his graduation from EHS in the spring of 1954, he studied hard to take the academy entrance exams. And he did well—even in math and science.

Midshipman McCain

Although Johnny McCain never considered *not* going to the Naval Academy, he was dreading it. Since he was a little boy he'd heard stories about the rigid discipline, the lack of privacy, the ruthless hazing. The academy was not a place that tolerated rebels.

McCain's life as a midshipman, a student at the academy, began on a day early in the summer of 1954, when his father drove him to the campus in Annapolis, Maryland. The buildings were gray granite with weathered copper roofs, set on three hundred grassy acres where the Severn River meets Chesapeake Bay. Together with his classmates, John McCain took an oath to "support and defend the Constitution of the United States." Now they were in for the next four years — unless they "bilged out," or had to leave, in disgrace.

At first the life of a midshipman didn't seem so bad to McCain. During the summer only a few upperclassmen were on campus to train the plebes, or first-year midshipmen. The plebes' schedule consisted mostly of sports, physical training, and learning to march in formation.

At the beginning of September, however, the rest of the upperclassmen arrived on campus and began to make life hard for John McCain and the other plebes. "Plebes" was short for "plebeians," meaning the lowest members of society. This wasn't just a name. Upperclassmen were allowed—actually *expected*—to treat the plebes like inferior beings.

Unless they were in their rooms, plebes had to remain at rigid attention all the time. Walking through the halls, sitting in class, or eating in the dining hall, their backs had to be ramrod straight, their eyes forward, and their chins tucked into an uncomfortable degree. This posture was called "bracing up." Plebes were required to be perfectly groomed at all times, and their rooms had to be kept in immaculate order. They had to memorize long, useless passages from a booklet titled *Reef Points*.

Upperclassmen watched the plebes carefully, trying to catch them breaking a rule. A common sight in the halls of the academy was an older midshipman barking questions at a plebe. While a plebe was being questioned and shouted at by an upperclassman, he was allowed only six answers. Those were: yes, sir; no, sir; aye, aye, sir; I'll find out, sir; no excuse, sir; or the answer to a specific question, often from *Reef Points*. They were supposed to have on the tips of their tongues dozens of facts, such as the number of panes of glass in the skylight of Memorial Hall—489.

If a plebe broke any of the rules, the upperclassman could punish him. Even if he followed all the rules perfectly, a plebe could still be bullied by the upperclassmen. The upperclassmen enjoyed putting plebes through humiliating and exhausting activities, such as crab-racing one another the length of the corridor. Crab-racing was done on all fours, except belly-up.

John McCain knew that his grandfather and his father had suffered the same hazing—in fact, hazing had been worse in the old days. When his father was a plebe in 1927, upperclassmen were allowed to punish plebes by beating them with sawed-off brooms. Jack, unusually small and young even for a plebe, was picked on more than most. But he'd endured the year of punishment without complaining.

There were good reasons, McCain concluded later,

for the harsh treatment of first-year midshipmen. By this means the US Naval Academy taught its midshipmen that their lives were no longer their own—they belonged to the navy. The plebes learned to take rank very seriously and to obey orders, no matter how senseless, without question.

Midshipmen at the academy weren't only attending college—they were also being trained as officers. One day they might command men in combat. If they couldn't stand the stress of plebe year, they probably couldn't stand the stress of fighting an actual war, either. In that case, it would be better for them and the navy for them to "bilge out." Before their four years at the academy were up, a quarter of McCain's class would be gone.

John McCain endured his plebe-year ordeal, but he let his tormentors see his contempt for them. He and his friends especially hated one upperclassman, given the name "Henry Witt" in McCain's memoir. Witt made John perform dozens of chores for him. For instance, McCain had to get up an hour early and come to Witt's room at five thirty every morning. On cold days, McCain was supposed to turn up the radiator so the room would be warm an hour later, when Witt got out of bed.

McCain resented most of all that Witt seemed to think John S. McCain III had been admitted to the academy because his family had influence. It was true that John's grandfather had been an admiral, and that his father was on his way to achieving the same rank. But John knew that he'd qualified for the academy on his own, by doing well on the entrance exams. However, he couldn't explain this to Witt, because it wasn't one of the six answers that plebes were allowed to give upperclassmen.

Under the grueling discipline of the Naval Academy, McCain's way of keeping his self-respect was to rebel. He got demerits every time he turned around, it seemed: for shoes not shined, for talking in the ranks, for a disorderly room. Breaking the rules and getting away with it was much harder here than it had been at Episcopal High School, but the challenge only made John more determined. He did obey the upperclassmen who made his life miserable, but he was careful to obey so as to show how much he despised them. He studied for his classes, but just enough to keep from flunking out.

McCain's father knew that John's grades were barely passing, and that he was piling up a stack of demerits. But most of the time he said nothing about it to John. As a midshipman, Jack McCain himself had continually gotten into trouble and received demerits. In his final year at the academy, Jack's battalion commander had given him a stern warning: if he got just one more demerit, he would not graduate with his class.

So Captain McCain understood where his son's rebellious behavior was coming from. However, once during John's second year at the academy, his father couldn't ignore the fact that his son was breaking the rules. That day John and his roommates, wearing only their underwear, were in the middle of a fierce water balloon fight when an officer knocked on the door. It was Jack McCain, come to visit his son.

The four midshipmen immediately snapped to attention in their wet underwear. "This room is in gross disorder," Captain McCain told them. In private a few minutes later, Jack McCain bawled John out. But John had the feeling that his father was only going through the motions of scolding him because he'd caught him in the act.

Later in life, Jack McCain cheerfully explained his justification for his own misbehavior at the academy. According to him, getting into trouble had its useful side. "You get to know people that you don't ordinarily know if you're one of the good boys. And sometimes the world's not always made up of all the good boys, either, not by a long shot." As for his son's conduct, Jack McCain really cared about only two things: whether John respected the honor code, and whether he would display courage and good character later, in the test of an actual war.

And in fact, it was only the rules that McCain rebelled against. In spite of his defiant attitude, he revered the academy's code of honor. According to the code, midshipmen did not lie, or cheat, or steal. They reported any other midshipman they found violating the code. It was the same code by which Jack McCain had lived his life, the code John had learned as a boy.

The midshipmen had a rule of their own, just as important as the formal rules of the academy: *never bilge a classmate*. In this sense, "bilge" meant to make your buddy look bad or otherwise let him down. Unless your classmate violated the code, you backed him up. This informal rule would stand the young officers in good stead after graduation, too. In combat, trusting one another would be a matter of life and death.

McCain's personal code of honor included fairness, and he had no respect for anyone who used his higher rank to abuse another. One day during McCain's second year at Annapolis, he was eating lunch in the mess hall, as the dining room was called. A "firstie," or fourth-year midshipman, sitting at the same table was in a bad mood. He began taking it out by picking on the steward waiting on their table.

Other classmates of McCain's simply kept silent or left the table, but McCain couldn't help saying, "Why don't you pick on someone your own size?" The firstie threatened to report McCain for insubordination, or challenging his authority. McCain coolly threatened to report *him* for breach of protocol, or incorrect conduct. The upperclassman was enraged, but he knew he was in the wrong and dropped the matter.

As at Episcopal High School, McCain became the ringleader of a band of rebellious classmates. They called themselves the "Bad Bunch." They were dedicated to breaking rules, and their favorite infraction was leaving the campus at night to drink beer and (they hoped) to meet girls. In fact, McCain was more successful than most of them at meeting girls, who seemed to be attracted to his reckless energy and high spirits.

The Bad Bunch was also dedicated to infuriating the commanding officer of their brigade, whom John

McCain called "Captain Ben Hart" in his memoirs. Since Captain Hart was unable to catch Midshipman McCain in the act of leaving campus, he punished him for everything else: sloppy dress, a messy room, a bad grade, or a smart remark. (McCain was already famous for smart remarks, as he would be for the rest of his life.) Captain Hart longed to get McCain and the rest of the Bad Bunch expelled from the academy.

But McCain, in spite of his rebellious behavior, was determined to stay and graduate. As he'd done in high school, he applied himself only in the classes he really liked—English and history. However, he made sure to get passing grades even in math. McCain's friends, working steadily and anxiously to keep up their own grades, were amazed at how he could cram for an exam at the last minute—and pass.

While John McCain was at the academy, he learned a piece of recent history that deeply impressed him: the story of General Billy Mitchell. Even at the beginning of the twentieth century, when the Wright brothers were just managing to fly the first airplane a few yards, Mitchell had understood how important airpower would become in warfare. Back before World War I, he predicted that aircraft, not battleships, would dominate war in the future. He urged the United States military to pour all its resources to developing an air force. Making enemies in the army, the navy, Congress, and the White House, Mitchell pushed to make the United States build its airpower.

Finally Mitchell crossed the line into insubordination. In 1925, after the navy dirigible *Shenandoah* crashed in a storm, Mitchell gave a public statement accusing army and navy leadership of "almost treasonable administration of the national defense." At that point, he was tried in a court-martial, found guilty, and suspended. He resigned his officer's commission. Billy Mitchell died in 1936, long before he was proved right by the events of World War II.

As John McCain progressed through his four years at the Naval Academy, his life as a midshipman gradually became more bearable. In June 1957 McCain and his classmates took a training cruise to Rio de Janeiro on the USS *Hunt*, an old destroyer. The purpose was to accustom them to life at sea and to show them how a naval warship was run.

The ship's commander, a former student of Jack McCain's, took John under his wing and gave him extra practice on the bridge. McCain was thrilled by the tricky challenge of commanding such a huge, unwieldy vessel. He'd always thought he'd rather become an aircraft pilot than a ship commander, but he almost changed his mind on the cruise.

During their leave in Rio, McCain and his friends partied for nine days straight. John met and fell in love with a beautiful Brazilian fashion model. To the envy of all the other midshipmen, she was smitten with him, too. Even after McCain had to sail north with his shipmates on the *Hunt*, he and the model carried on a long-distance romance for several months.

The training voyage gave McCain a good feeling about himself and the navy, and he actually began studying hard and behaving himself during his last year at the academy. Captain Hart had not changed his mind about Midshipman McCain, however. Halfway through the year, Hart informed McCain that he had put him in last place in his class. In the spring, Hart unfairly gave McCain seventy-five demerits for a minor offense, "Room in gross disorder," usually worth only fifteen demerits. McCain was now dangerously close to the level of demerits that would get him expelled before graduation.

Eventually Hart's injustice came to the attention of the superintendent of the academy, and McCain's demerits were reduced to a manageable level. But a month or so later, another close call occurred. Captain

Hart discovered a forbidden television set hidden in the room McCain shared with three other students. Possession of an electric appliance was a serious offense, enough to get McCain expelled. Captain Hart was sure he had McCain at last. But then one of the other co-owners of the TV set, a midshipman with only a few demerits, gallantly claimed ownership and saved his buddy's career.

And so on the bright, sunny day of June 4, 1958, John McCain graduated from the Naval Academy. He and his classmates were midshipmen no longer — they were ensigns, the lowest rank of commissioned officers in the navy. President Dwight D. Eisenhower, Supreme Commander of the Allied Forces during World War II, gave the commencement speech. The president also personally presented their diplomas to those who were graduating with distinction, beginning with John Poindexter, first in the class of 1958.

John McCain was not one of the distinguished ones that day. In fact, he was fifth from the bottom in a class of nearly nine hundred. However, his low standing didn't bother him much. After all, his grandfather had graduated in the bottom quarter of his class, and his father had barely squeaked through. And they'd both gone on to have distinguished careers as navy officers.

Chapter 4

Naval Aviator

Ensign McCain spent his vacation after graduation traveling around Europe. In August 1958 he reported to the Naval Air Station at Pensacola, Florida, for flight training. He was following in the footsteps of his grandfather, who had earned his navy pilot's wings at the age of fifty-two. McCain's father had originally planned to become a navy pilot, but before he graduated from the academy, he was judged "not physically qualified" for aviation school.

John McCain liked flying, as he'd thought he would, but he wasn't dedicated to flying like some pilots. It was just part of an enjoyable way of life. Now that he was out from under the extreme discipline of the Naval Academy, he gave free rein to his rowdy tendencies.

McCain drove a flashy sports car, a Corvette. He

went out on lots of dates with lots of women. He and his buddies spent a good part of their free time at a local bar, Trader John's. To the admiration of his friends, McCain dated a young woman who worked as an "exotic dancer" at Trader John's.

From Pensacola, McCain went on to advanced flight training at Corpus Christi, on the coast of Texas. He still saw no reason to change his wild ways. He roomed with Chuck Larson, a classmate and good friend from the academy, and they kept their quarters in what the navy termed "gross disorder."

One day, as John McCain was flying his A-1 Skyraider solo over Corpus Christi Bay to practice water landings, his engine quit. The plane crashed in the bay, knocking him unconscious. Luckily, he revived, forced open the canopy of the plane, and swam up. Miraculously, McCain's only injury was a sore back. He went to yet another party that night.

At the same time, there was also a serious side to John McCain. In between flight training and wild partying, he found time for some heavy reading. Larson was surprised one day to find his roommate reading Edward Gibbon's *Decline and Fall of the Roman Empire*, a history classic written in the eighteenth century. McCain's father had told him it was a book a naval officer should know about, and so McCain read it—all three volumes. Gibbon believed that the Roman Empire had collapsed because the Romans had grown soft and lazy, no longer willing to fight and sacrifice for the empire.

As McCain's flight training continued, he went on several cruises in the Mediterranean. He learned to take off from and land on an aircraft carrier. McCain liked being at sea on a carrier, and he liked flying the Skyraider, a propeller-driven attack bomber that had first been used in the Korean War. He loved the idea of himself as a bold, dashing hero of the air. At last, he felt, he was living like the characters in the adventure stories he'd read as a boy.

During his trips to Europe, John McCain took a few voluntary courses in the techniques of "evasion and escape" if shot down over enemy territory. In one exercise, the pilots were released in the middle of the Black Forest in Germany with only a map and a few C rations, the military's canned food. The pilots' goal was to escape the area without being caught by either the army or any German civilians. McCain and his buddy enjoyed the adventure, and after five days of evading "capture," they reached the "safe" goal.

More sobering was a conversation McCain had a

few days later with a Korean War veteran. This air force officer had spent time in a North Korean prison, where he was held for a long period in solitary confinement. McCain was amazed that the man had been able to keep his sanity. John McCain was always at his happiest in a crowd of people; by himself, he tended to get more and more restless and uneasy. He could imagine—or thought he could imagine—what a grim test of character it would be, week after week of never seeing or talking to another human being.

In October 1962, unaware that a world crisis was building, McCain returned from one of his practice missions in the Mediterranean. He and the other pilots flew their planes from their carrier, the USS *Enterprise*, to the air base near Norfolk, Virginia. A few days later they were surprised to be ordered back to the *Enterprise*, which then headed toward the Caribbean Sea.

On the way to the Caribbean, the pilots listened in amazement to President John F. Kennedy on the radio. The president informed the country that the Soviet Union was placing nuclear missiles on Cuba—Cuba, only ninety miles from the tip of Florida. These missiles could reach most of the major American cities.

President Kennedy responded with a military

blockade of Cuba, demanding that the Soviets remove their missiles. The world edged terrifyingly close to nuclear war. For five days McCain and his squadron waited on high alert, expecting to be ordered into action from their carrier at any time. Then the United States and the Soviet Union began negotiations to resolve the crisis. This was not, after all, to be McCain's first experience of combat.

McCain continued his training missions. On one of his last trips to the Mediterranean, he almost met personal disaster again. Flying too low over southern Spain, he accidentally knocked down some power lines. However, he wasn't hurt, and soon afterward he graduated from flight school. He was now a naval aviator. After moving back to Pensacola, McCain worked as a flight instructor at the naval air base.

During the four years since his graduation from Annapolis, John McCain had begun to think beyond the next party. He realized that he wanted to pursue a career in the navy, and he wanted to do more than just fly planes. He intended to be a leader—to command a squadron or an aircraft carrier. In order to be considered for such a position, he needed to fly combat missions.

It seemed that he would get his chance, as international tensions worsened. At this time the United

States was more worried than ever that Communism, as practiced by the Soviet Union and China, could take over the world. Eastern Europe was under Communist rule. In Asia, North Korea and North Vietnam, as well as China (except for the island of Taiwan), had Communist governments. Hoping to stop this trend in Vietnam, the United States was supporting the anti-communist South Vietnam government with money—and more and more military troops.

In November 1963 President Kennedy was assassinated, and his vice president, Lyndon B. Johnson, became president. The next summer, 1964, Congress passed the Tonkin Gulf Resolution, which gave President Johnson war powers in Vietnam. Ensign McCain, eager for combat duty, lobbied influential officers for the chance to be sent to Vietnam. He transferred to the air station at Meridian, Mississippi, to work as a flight instructor and get ready for combat. The airfield there, McCain Field, had been named after his grandfather.

Meanwhile, McCain was seriously dating Carol Shepp of Philadelphia. He'd known Carol since his Annapolis days; in fact, she had married one of his classmates. She was now divorced, with two little boys.

John McCain and Carol were married in July 1965,

and shortly afterward John adopted her sons, Doug and Andy. In September 1966 their daughter, Sidney Ann McCain, was born. Although McCain was a serious family man and delighted in all three of his children, this didn't change his resolve to go into combat.

McCain wasn't afraid—after all, a pilot's life was dangerous, even without combat. He had already had two close calls: the time he crashed into Corpus Christi Bay during flight training, and the time he flew into the power lines over Spain. While he was stationed at Meridian, another pilot had broken his leg ejecting from his plane. The pilot survived the crash, but then blood pooled in his broken leg, and he went into shock and died.

In the fall of 1965, as McCain was flying from Philadelphia to his base in Meridian, Mississippi, his engine quit. He ejected before the plane crashed, and he wasn't hurt. But he worried that another accident might prevent him from winning glory in Vietnam and eventually achieving a command post.

The more deeply the United States became involved in the war in Vietnam, the more seriously divided Americans were over whether the country should be spending money and losing soldiers' lives there. On one side, the "hawks" believed that the

United States had a right and a duty to intervene in Vietnam with military force, to stop the spread of Communism. On the other side, "doves" believed that the conflict in Vietnam was basically a civil war, and the United States had no business interfering. This was very different from World War II, when almost all Americans had been convinced that we were fighting for our country's survival.

Although the draft was still in effect in the 1960s, and all able-bodied young American men were required to serve in the military, more than half of them managed to avoid it. Men in college or graduate school, married men, and especially married men with children were exempt from the draft. Beyond that, some men became conscientious objectors or simply left the country for Canada. A few went to prison in protest against the war.

For John McCain, there was no reason to question the war. He had chosen a military career, and soldiers fight where they are ordered to fight. Proud of his father's and grandfather's service in World War II, he couldn't imagine anything nobler than following their example. As President Theodore Roosevelt once said, "Aggressive fighting for the right is the noblest sport the world affords." John McCain remembered his grandfather's words to his father, the last time they saw each other: that it was a privilege to die for principles and country.

In the fall of 1966, John McCain said goodbye to Carol and their three children and flew to Jacksonville, Florida, to join his squadron on the aircraft carrier *Forrestal*. The squadron would leave that summer for the Tonkin Gulf, an arm of the South China Sea off the coast of North Vietnam. While they were stationed at Jacksonville, McCain trained with the A-4 Skyhawk, the small jet bomber that was replacing the propeller-driven A-1 Skyraider.

In May 1967 McCain's father, now a vice admiral in the navy, was appointed commander in chief of the United States Naval Forces in Europe. Jack and Roberta McCain were based in London, and Carol moved to Europe with the children, intending to send them to an American school in Garmisch, Germany, while John was away. His tour of duty was supposed to last less than a year.

The *Forrestal* arrived at the Tonkin Gulf in July, and John McCain and his fellow attack pilots began flying bombing missions over North Vietnam. Every morning Skyhawks were catapulted from the deck of the carrier and headed north with their cargo of bombs. On July 29, McCain prepared as usual for the day's mission. He had just settled into the cockpit of his plane when a missile, accidentally set off from another fighter plane, struck his fuel tank.

John McCain barely had time to burst out of his plane, jump into the fire that instantly engulfed the Skyhawk, and roll to safety on the deck of the aircraft carrier. In those split seconds, the fire spread from plane to plane, exploding bombs, setting off missiles, and igniting fuel tanks. The crew of the *Forrestal* fought the flames through the day and into the night. Finally they managed to put the fire out completely, saving the ship. But 134 men lost their lives.

The *Forrestal*, badly damaged, had to return to the United States for extensive repairs. The fighter pilots in its squadron were expected to return too, but John McCain was reluctant. He had come to Vietnam to fly combat missions, and he wanted to complete his tour of duty. When an officer from another carrier, the *Oriskany*, asked for volunteers, John gladly transferred to the other ship.

At this point McCain was given a few weeks' leave, and he flew to Europe to see his parents and Carol and the children. After his narrow escape from death in the *Forrestal* fire, they were especially grateful to be together. John and Carol McCain and their children enjoyed a vacation on the Mediterranean before he returned to the war.

As John McCain reported to the *Oriskany* in September 1967, more and more Americans came to believe that the war was wrong. The antiwar movement grew, putting on large public demonstrations and pressing Congress and President Johnson to withdraw from Vietnam. In October about thirty-five thousand "doves" gathered outside the Pentagon, the headquarters of the Department of Defense, to demand an end to the war.

Meanwhile, President Johnson had ordered an escalation of the bombing of North Vietnam. That made sense to McCain and his fellow pilots. They thought that the president and his secretary of defense, Robert S. McNamara, had been too cautious so far. They believed that the more aggressively the United States fought, the sooner the war would be over.

Of course, increased bombing meant increased danger for the pilots. The reason the *Oriskany* needed volunteers was that they had lost so many pilots. During 1967, a third of them were killed or captured in bombing missions. McCain knew the danger—he could see for himself that whenever the squadron flew out on a raid, it returned with pilots missing. But like most of the pilots, his way of dealing with constant danger was to put on a "game face."

The morning of October 26, a friend on the *Oriskany* warned John McCain to be careful. "You don't have to worry about me," was his cocky answer. Shortly afterward he took off from the carrier in his single-seat Skyhawk with the rest of his squadron. It was his twenty-third bombing raid, but it would be his first over Hanoi, the capital of North Vietnam. His assignment was to bomb the thermal plant on the edge of a small lake in the middle of the city.

At that time Hanoi was the best-defended city in the history of air warfare. It was well supplied with radar equipment to detect enemy planes, and with surface-to-air missiles, or SAMs, to shoot them down. However, the American bombers were equipped with warning systems to alert them to approaching missiles.

Just as McCain was about to release his bombs over the thermal plant, his defensive equipment signaled that a SAM was speeding straight toward him. But McCain had confidence in his fast, nimble Skyhawk, so he stayed over the target long enough to drop the bombs. The next instant the missile tore off his wing. He had barely enough time to eject before his plane plummeted toward the ground.

Chapter 5

Prisoner in the Hanoi Hilton

As John McCain ejected over Hanoi, he collided with his damaged plane, breaking both arms and his right knee. His parachute opened just before he landed in the shallow lake, and he sank to the bottom. He kicked off with his left leg, surfaced, and started to sink again. His fifty pounds of flight gear would drown him if his life vest didn't inflate.

McCain tried to reach for the life vest cord—but his arms would not move. Again he sank to the bottom and kicked off with his left leg. Unable to use his hands, he inflated his life vest by pulling the cord with his teeth.

A man swam out from the shore and pulled McCain out of the lake. The citizens of Hanoi crowded around, hitting and kicking the American pilot. As McCain remarked years later, he could understand why they were angry. After all, he had been dropping bombs on their city.

One man smashed a rifle butt into McCain's shoulder, breaking the joint. Others kicked him, hit him, spat on him, and jabbed him with bayonets. A nurse tried to protect him and splinted his broken limbs with bamboo. Finally an army truck arrived and took him away to Hoa Lo Prison, on the other side of Hanoi.

From the outside, Hoa Lo looked like a run-down nineteenth-century French hotel—except for the towering gates. Inside, it was a grim and terrifying prison. The French colonialist government had held and tortured Vietnamese prisoners there, and now the North Vietnamese were using Hoa Lo as their main detention site for American prisoners of war. The Americans, with grim sarcasm, called it the "Hanoi Hilton."

McCain was set down in a filthy cell, and for several days he was kept there without medical treatment. He drifted from agonizing pain into unconsciousness and then back to pain again. From time to time interrogators appeared, demanding military information. But McCain would only give his name, rank, serial number, and date of birth, as all members of the US military were taught to do. His interrogators shouted at him and hit him, but he was so badly injured that any mistreatment caused him to lose consciousness again.

John McCain was fed twice a day, but he was unable to keep food down, and he lay in his own vomit and filth. His condition worsened until his captors thought he was going to die, and so did McCain. His broken right knee was swollen to the size of a football, reminding him of the pilot in Meridian who had died of the same kind of injury.

Then the North Vietnamese discovered that John McCain was the son of an important admiral in the US Navy, and they rushed him to the hospital. The hospital room, infested with mosquitoes and rats, wasn't much cleaner than the prison cell, but at least he received transfusions and shots. He managed to keep some food down. As soon as McCain seemed well enough to recover, the interrogators returned day after day. If he did not provide military information, they told him, they would not provide the further medical treatment he needed.

John McCain lay helpless, unable to even feed himself, but his rebellious spirit was as strong as ever. When the Vietnamese interrogators pressed him to give more information, he finally told them he would reveal the names of the other pilots in his squadron.

Then he glibly recited a string of names. The reason he could rattle these names off the top of his head was that he was an avid sports fan—they were the names of the Green Bay Packers football team's offensive line.

But now that his captors knew that John McCain was the son of an admiral, they were more interested in using him for propaganda than for information. They invited a French journalist to come into the hospital and interview the downed American pilot on film. By this time McCain was in a plaster cast for his badly broken right arm, although it hadn't been set properly.

For the interview, McCain was placed in a clean, well-equipped hospital room. The Vietnamese officers, off camera, kept telling him what to say: that he was grateful to the Vietnamese people for treating him so well, that he was sorry for his war crimes, and that he wanted the war to end so that he could go home. McCain refused, although he did send a message to Carol: "I'm going to get well. I love her, and hope to see her soon." The interview ended, and he was returned to the room with the mosquitoes and rats.

The prison authorities weren't happy with John McCain. Unless he changed his attitude, they threatened, they would not give him the operation on his knee that he needed. In early December the surgery was performed anyway, but it was crudely done, and he was in great pain. Besides, McCain had a fever and dysentery, and he had lost fifty pounds from his already trim frame since his capture.

The Vietnamese still had plans to use McCain for propaganda, and they didn't want him to die. At his request, they took him to another prison in Hanoi, nicknamed "the Plantation" by the American prisoners. There they put him in a cell with two air force pilots, George "Bud" Day and Norris Overly.

By now McCain was in such poor condition that Day and Overly were sure he was going to die. Bud Day was in bad shape himself, having been severely injured when his plane was shot down, and then tortured by the Vietnamese. But Overly was able to clean their new cellmate, feed him, and massage his leg—and McCain began to recover. He talked nonstop, overjoyed to be with fellow Americans and eager to learn everything they could tell him. Only a few weeks after his transfer, he was up and getting around on crutches.

Not long after that, in February 1968 the Vietnamese released Norris Overly, along with two other POWs, to the Americans. It was the first time they'd released any American prisoners of war. Day and McCain advised

Overly not to go. According to the Code of Conduct for US armed forces, prisoners must be released in the order in which they were captured. This was only fair, when many men had already endured years in Vietnamese prisons. The first American, Everett Alvarez, had been captured in August 1964.

Overly decided to leave anyway, and some of the remaining POWs criticized him bitterly. But John McCain couldn't be too harsh. After all, Overly had saved his life. "I thought him a good man then, as I do today," he wrote later.

For himself, though, McCain was determined not to be released early, because he knew it would harm American morale. Aside from the Code of Conduct, "Never bilge on a buddy" was right near the top in McCain's private code of honor. If he accepted early release, he would be letting his fellow prisoners down.

An excuse might have been made for John McCain to go home before other prisoners. Although no longer actually dying, he was still badly injured and suffering from dysentery. But he would not let the Vietnamese use him as propaganda, pointing to the admiral's son who had cooperated with the enemy.

One day a group of Vietnamese officials approached McCain's cell to offer him amnesty, or pardon for his "crimes." McCain began to scream at them, so loudly that prisoners up and down the cellblock could hear, that he would not take early release. The other POWs listened with delight to the stream of obscenities McCain spewed out at the officials. One of the prisoners said later, "You can't imagine the example John set for the rest of the camp."

The American prisoners were hungry for news, but the only news they were allowed was propaganda designed to weaken their morale. A public address system piped in cheerful broadcasts about North Vietnamese victories. The PA system also relayed any discouraging news from the United States, especially about the growing antiwar movement. For real news, the prisoners depended on recently captured Americans.

The POWs were forbidden to communicate with one another, but they risked punishment to exchange gossip, lame jokes, and every scrap of news they could gather. They discussed all kinds of subjects, including US politics. They were disappointed in President Johnson, although they would never admit it to the Vietnamese.

In March 1968 Johnson had ordered a halt to the bombing of North Vietnam, and the POWs thought this was a mistake. They had high hopes for Ronald

Reagan, now the new governor of California and perhaps president one day. Reagan had spoken out strongly against the war protesters.

The American prisoners entertained one another by giving the prison officials insulting nicknames. The short, fat prison camp commander was "the Bug"; one officer was "Chihuahua"; "Soft Soap" was the interrogator who pretended to be the prisoners' friend. Another pastime for the POWs was lively contests as to who could kill the most mosquitoes. One day McCain and Day together counted some four hundred kills.

About a month after Overly left, Bud Day was moved to another prison. John McCain spent the next two years straight in solitary confinement. His cell had a wooden board for a bed. A bare lightbulb in the ceiling shone day and night, so the guards could observe the prisoner. The roof of the prison was tin, there was no ventilation, and in the summer the heat was suffocating. But the worst thing McCain suffered in prison—worse than his crippling injuries and physical pain, worse than being sick and half-starved, worse than the filthy cells and miserable food—was being alone.

In solitary confinement, McCain and the other

POWs developed amazing skills at communicating. They tapped out messages in code through the walls separating their cells. They talked through the walls, using their drinking mugs to amplify the sound. Even a small gesture, like a thumbs-up as a guard escorted a man past another prisoner's cell, lifted their spirits tremendously.

John McCain spent many long hours with nothing to do but think. He kept his mind healthy by going over the books he'd read before his capture, especially history books. In solitude, he was able to reconstruct whole books in his mind. He rethought American foreign policy, discussing with himself what mistakes the United States had made.

Even before he was captured, McCain and his fellow pilots had criticized the way the Vietnam War was being run. President Lyndon B. Johnson was concerned that a too-vigorous attack on North Vietnam might cause China or the Soviet Union to use nuclear weapons, so he insisted on approving the bombing targets himself. The pilots felt that some of the targets they bombed were unimportant, while other targets, which they were not allowed to bomb, might have helped win the war. Being well-trained soldiers, the pilots followed their orders—risking their lives as they did so—but their doubts about their leadership were not good for their morale.

In April 1968 the POWs learned from Vietnamese propaganda broadcasts about the assassination of Dr. Martin Luther King. In June 1968 they heard about the assassination of Senator Robert Kennedy. That same year, on July 4, McCain's father was appointed commander in chief of all US forces in the Pacific. But McCain didn't find this out until a year later. And although the United States made the first successful manned moon landing in 1969, McCain and the other prisoners didn't hear about that until three years later.

In May 1968 the United States began peace talks with Vietnam in Paris. The POWs' hopes soared, and they were sure they'd be released soon. But the talks dragged on for months, then years, seeming to go nowhere. The prisoners learned not to get too hopeful, telling one another, "Steady strain." They made fun of POWs who found bright hope in the tiniest little signs, like unexpected carrots in their watery soup.

During the first year or so of McCain's captivity, his captors tried hard to make him confess to committing war crimes, and to persuade him to accept early release. The Vietnamese stepped up the harshness of their interrogations, beating him three or four times a week for months on end. When this mistreatment didn't change his mind, they tried other forms of torture. McCain was made to stand in one position for hours at a time, or his arms were tied behind his back and the ropes tightened to excruciating pain.

But only once, in the first weeks of this period, did his captors break his spirit. After three days of being beaten every few hours, until his left arm was re-broken and his ribs were cracked, he was afraid he couldn't hold out any longer. He tried to kill himself, but the guards prevented him.

On the fourth day of beatings, he gave up and agreed to sign a confession. The confession, written by an interrogator, stated that McCain had committed "black crimes" against the Vietnamese people and was grateful for the humane treatment he had received in Hanoi. The North Vietnamese valued world opinion, and they wanted other nations to believe they were following the Third Geneva Convention, adopted by the United Nations in 1949. This international agreement explained in detail how prisoners of war must be decently fed and housed, given medical treatment, allowed letters and packages from home, and so on. McCain and other POWs found some dark humor in the fact that they were being tortured into saying how well they were treated.

Later, after further beatings, John McCain read his confession aloud into a tape recorder. None of his fellow prisoners blamed him for breaking down and confessing, and the choice of words such as "black crimes" and "air pirate" made it clear that his confession was forced. But McCain blamed himself, and he was deeply ashamed of giving in.

John McCain never broke down again. Through the following months and years of being beaten, tortured, and half-starved, he only grew tougher. Defying his captors cheered him up, even when he knew his defiance would result in worse punishment. He was sustained by the knowledge that he was one of a community of soldiers, and that they all had faith in one another.

One reason the Vietnamese wanted to prevent the prisoners from talking to one another was to disrupt their military discipline. As soldiers, McCain and his fellow prisoners relied on advice and encouragement from their senior officers. It was vitally important for them to know who the senior ranking officers, or SROs, in their prison block were and to turn to them for guidance. That way, although they might look like filthy, wretched prisoners, in their minds they were still soldiers in a disciplined military unit. That made all the difference.

It was during these hardest months of being tortured that John McCain discovered what his deepest values were. He'd always thought his self-respect depended on his independent, rebellious attitude. He'd striven for glory—*self*-glory. But now, reaching out for something larger than himself, he found a solid faith in his country, and in all the Americans, living and dead, who had dedicated themselves to defending it.

McCain thought about his grandfather, who had given his last drop of vitality in fighting World War II, and dropped dead four days after the Japanese surrender. He thought about his father, who had steadfastly guided his submarine crew to the edge of suffocation and back. They had believed that the United States, the country they served, had a special calling in the world. They believed that their common destiny was well worth their sacrifice.

In August 1969 the North Vietnamese suffered a wave of unfavorable publicity, when it was revealed to the world how badly they had mistreated American POWs. On September 2, 1969, Ho Chi Minh, president of

North Vietnam, died of a heart attack. After these two events, treatment of the American prisoners improved somewhat. John McCain was transferred back to Ho Loa Prison, the Hanoi Hilton, and placed in room 7.

When a marine fighter pilot named Orson Swindle was moved into room 6, McCain eagerly introduced himself through the wall. First he tapped out his name, and then he tapped out a stupid joke. Listening in disbelief, Swindle thought that McCain must be mentally unhinged from his ordeal. However, before long they became good friends.

After John McCain had spent almost three years, off and on, in solitary confinement, he was transferred on Christmas 1970 to a large room with almost fifty other Americans. McCain was giddy with delight, especially when he saw that one of the others was Bud Day, his cellmate shortly after capture. McCain would always remember this day as the happiest day of his life.

The POWs nicknamed this section of Hoa Lo "Camp Unity." With such companionship, the men felt they could stand anything. They invented many ways to occupy their time and entertain one another. John McCain taught a class in social studies, based on his longtime reading of history books.

One of McCain's best friends in Camp Unity was Orson Swindle, with whom he'd exchanged messages tapped on the wall between their cells. Swindle also loved good books, and together they taught a course in English and American literature. McCain had always been a good storyteller, but now he developed his skills even further. In great detail, with much dramatic expression, he told the men the stories of his favorite novels. These favorites included, of course, Ernest Hemingway's *For Whom the Bell Tolls*, which he'd read countless times.

John McCain and Orson Swindle also regularly presented "Movie Night." At these events they told, again as dramatically as possible, the stories of all the movies they could remember. *Stalag 17*, a classic about POWs in a German prison camp during World War II, was a big hit with the men. Naturally McCain told *Viva Zapata!*, beloved since his boyhood, about the Mexican rebel struggling against overwhelming odds. The western *One-Eyed Jacks*, which also starred Marlon Brando, was also a favorite with the POWs.

On Christmas 1971 the American prisoners celebrated the season with all their resources. A well-rehearsed choir led the singing of Christmas carols. John McCain, appointed as chaplain, got hold of a

Bible long enough to scribble down passages from the Christmas story. He read them aloud in their Christmas night service.

Peace negotiations had been on again, off again since John McCain was captured, but now there were signs that the war might really come to an end. The American prisoners were cheered in April 1972, when President Richard Nixon ordered the bombing of North Vietnam to start up again. The POWs had long felt that the United States was fighting this war halfheartedly, and they believed that now the North Vietnamese would be more willing to engage in talks.

The following Christmas, 1972, the Americans cheered and slapped one another on the back as Hanoi itself was bombed unmercifully. They themselves were in Hanoi, and the American bombs could have fallen on them. But the POWs were elated that the United States was attacking with serious force. "Let's hear it for Richard Nixon!" they shouted.

At the beginning of 1973, an end to the war was negotiated. There was a cease-fire on both sides. The United States withdrew its troops from Vietnam, and prisoners of war were exchanged. However, North Vietnam was allowed to continue supplying materials to Communist troops in South Vietnam.

The American POWs were released in the order in which they had been captured. Finally, on March 14, 1973, John McCain walked across the tarmac at Gia Lam Airport and climbed aboard a US Air Force plane.

The aircraft was a big green C-141, a workhorse transport plane. To McCain and his fellow POWs, it looked so beautiful that tears came to their eyes. They fondly dubbed it the "Hanoi Taxi."

Even on the plane, John McCain and the men released with him hardly dared to believe they were free now. They had been prisoners for too long, telling one another, "Steady strain." It was only when the plane crossed the invisible line between Vietnam air space and international air space that they burst out cheering.

Chapter 6

Moving On

When John McCain arrived at the Jacksonville airport a few days later, Carol and their three children came to meet the husband and father they hadn't seen for nearly six years. Sidney, a baby when McCain was shot down, knew him only from family pictures. She was overwhelmed when he squeezed her tight and didn't want to let her go.

The whole country, it seemed, wanted to welcome the POWs home as heroes. A few years before McCain's release, many Americans had started wearing inexpensive metal bracelets, engraved with the name, rank, and date of capture or reported missing in action of a prisoner of war, to show support for these soldiers. When the POWs returned from Vietnam, they were amazed to see crowds of cheering strangers wearing bracelets for *them*.

In May, President Richard Nixon held a reception at the White House for John McCain and other POWs. The Senate was beginning hearings on the Watergate break-in, and the Nixon administration was in serious trouble. But to the former POWs, President Nixon was the hero they'd cheered for ordering the resumed bombing of Hanoi.

John McCain was thin, silver-haired at the age of only thirty-six, and on crutches. But he proudly wore his ceremonial uniform, his navy "dress whites," for the reception. His POW friend Bud Day, who had seen McCain on the point of death in their Hanoi cell, thought he looked pretty good in contrast.

During that spring, Ronald and Nancy Reagan invited John and Carol McCain to dinner at their home in Pacific Palisades, California. Governor Reagan had taken a special interest in the Vietnam POWs since the beginning of the war, and now he wanted to hear every detail of McCain's imprisonment. At first McCain was reluctant to take up so much of the governor's time, but at the Reagans' urging, he held them spellbound for hours with his stories—exciting, funny, appalling, heartbreaking. McCain was thrilled and touched that Governor Reagan, a leader he'd admired for years, would honor him and pay him so much attention.

In May, *U.S. News & World Report* published John McCain's account of his five and a half years as a POW in Vietnam. McCain was a celebrity, which embarrassed him and his POW friends. "Basically we feel that we are just average American Navy, Marine, and Air Force pilots who got shot down. Anybody else in our place would have performed just as well."

Like many Vietnam veterans, John McCain faced big challenges in adjusting to life back in the United States. Fortunately, he never suffered from post-traumatic stress disorder (PTSD), as many veterans did. Some were afflicted with flashbacks, in which they relived the horrors of imprisonment or combat. Some were so anxious or depressed that they were no longer able to work.

However, McCain's physical injuries, together with years of harsh treatment in prison, had left him somewhat disabled. He couldn't lift his arms above his head, and Carol had to comb his hair for him. He could barely bend his right knee.

Then there was family life, quite a big adjustment in itself. McCain's adopted sons, Doug and Andy, were glad to have their father home, but his daughter, Sidney, didn't remember him at all. His wife, Carol, had changed as much as John had in his absence. She'd almost died in a car accident in 1969, and her injuries had left her four inches shorter. And although Carol and the children had missed John and longed for his return, they were used to being a family without him.

There was no one at home, even those John McCain loved most, who could really understand what he'd been through in Vietnam. When he'd said good-bye to Bud Day, Orson Swindle, and the rest who had suffered and endured Vietnam with him, he felt a strange loneliness. He would see his POW friends back in the United States, but things would never be the same again.

Luckily for McCain's postwar adjustment, he wasn't one to live in the past. He'd always been a restless, impatient person, and as a navy kid, he'd grown up expecting not to stay long in any one place. Like his favorite president, Theodore Roosevelt, he thought life should be "forward motion." As McCain expressed it later in his book *Worth the Fighting For*, "Keep moving if you want to love life, and keep your troubles well behind you."

One thing John McCain was not willing to leave behind was his life as a navy pilot. The main problem was his right knee, which had been smashed when his plane was shot down and then further injured by clumsy surgery in the Hanoi hospital and years of neglect. He could only bend the knee five degrees. In order to work the brakes in a plane again, he'd have to be able to bend the knee at a right angle, ninety degrees. The doctors told him that he would never fly again.

Undiscouraged, McCain endured several surgeries on his right knee, and then launched into a program of painful physical therapy. While he slowly improved his physical fitness, he studied at the National War College in Washington, DC. He chose his own subject: the Vietnam War.

McCain had played a part in this chapter of history, and now he wanted to understand everything about Vietnam. He studied the culture, the politics, and the long history that led up to the United States' involvement. More than fifty-eight thousand US soldiers, some of them his good friends, had died in the Vietnam War. The United States had spent $120 billion (more than $800 billion in 2018 dollars) on the conflict. Yet the supposed goal of the war, saving Vietnam from Communist domination, had not been accomplished.

At the end of the year, McCain was satisfied that he understood what had happened in the Vietnam War and why. Now his habit of moving forward, always forward, in life stood him in good stead. Perhaps he had reason to hate the protesters of the war, the American draft evaders, or the Hanoi prison guards, but he chose not to waste his life in bitterness. He had been through horrors in prison, but he chose not to dwell on them. "You move on," he explained later in his memoir *Faith of My Fathers*, "remembering the good, while the bad grows obscure in the distance."

Many Vietnam POWs would never forgive the war protesters. The worst of those, they felt, was the actress Jane Fonda, who had been outspoken against the war from the beginning. Early in 1972 she won the Academy Award for Best Actress, and that summer she visited Hanoi. There she posed, smiling, with an antiaircraft gun. She gave an address on Radio Hanoi, urging US pilots to stop flying bombing missions in Vietnam. She even reported confidently that the American POWs were being well treated. Jane Fonda had asked to meet with John McCain; he refused, knowing that he would be used only for propaganda.

But the people McCain criticized the most harshly were the American politicians and generals in charge of the US forces in Vietnam. In his opinion, our leaders had mismanaged the war. Their real war crime, he felt, was sending young men off to die when the country was not wholehearted about fighting the war.

By a cruel coincidence, McCain's own father, Admiral John S. McCain Jr., had been commander in chief of the US forces in the Pacific during McCain's years in prison. This did not mean that Admiral McCain could choose to conduct the war as he thought best—he had to follow orders from Washington. It also didn't mean that he could do anything to protect his son. Admiral McCain's strict code of honor told him that his son was only one of hundreds of POWs, only one of hundreds of thousands of soldiers, and he was equally responsible for all these men.

Roberta McCain later told her son that during the war, his father had prayed every evening on his knees, in agony over what he knew his son must be suffering. Every Christmas for three years, Admiral McCain had visited the DMZ, the demilitarized zone between North and South Vietnam, and stood staring bleakly northward. It was the closest he could get to Hanoi — and his namesake in the Hanoi Hilton.

During the school year 1973–74, while John McCain was studying at the War College, the Watergate scandal was snowballing. By the spring of 1974, the US House of Representatives had begun to consider impeaching President Nixon — sending him to the US Senate to be tried for misconduct in office. His alleged misconduct included covering up crimes committed by members of his staff.

In August 1974 Richard M. Nixon became the first president of the United States to resign. McCain was sorry; he respected Nixon for ordering the bombing campaign that hastened the end of the war, and he liked him for welcoming the POWs back to the United States. McCain felt that the Watergate scandal had been overblown by the president's political enemies.

In the spring of 1974, Governor Reagan invited John McCain to Sacramento, California, to speak at his annual prayer breakfast. McCain moved the audience, including Ronald Reagan, to tears with a story from his POW years. It was about a time he was in solitary confinement, in complete despair, and found an inspirational message scratched on the wall by another prisoner: "I believe in God, the Father Almighty."

By the summer of 1974, through month after month of extremely painful physical therapy, John McCain had inched his right knee back to flexibility. Finally able to bend the knee ninety degrees, he nagged the navy doctors into letting him go back to flying. He still had a slight limp, he still couldn't tie his own shoes or comb his own hair, and he had some trouble working the gears in the cockpit of a plane. In an emergency, he might not have been able to push open the canopy of his plane, as he had over Corpus Christi Bay during his flight training, and over Hanoi on his last bombing mission. But he was officially cleared for flight status.

Late in the fall of 1974, John McCain returned to Vietnam as a guest of the South Vietnamese government, which was still fighting North Vietnam. He was to help celebrate National Day in Saigon, the capital of South Vietnam. John thought the trip would help him put his Vietnam years in perspective, especially after his studies at the War College.

While he was in Saigon, McCain asked to be

taken to a prison. He'd heard accusations from pro-testers of the Vietnam War that the South Vietnamese mistreated *their* POWs, and he wanted to see for him-self. Sure enough, McCain found that the conditions in the South Vietnamese prison were at least as grim as those he'd suffered in the Hanoi Hilton. He wasn't surprised, the following April, when the Vietnam War ended in defeat for the South. In 1976 North Vietnam and South Vietnam were reunited as the Socialist Republic of Vietnam.

Returning to active duty in the navy, John McCain was assigned to the naval base at Jacksonville, where in 1976 he became the commanding officer of his squadron. Then, in 1977, because he was personable and widely known as an ex-POW, the navy assigned him to the Senate liaison office. This post wasn't sup-posed to be an important one, and usually the Senate liaison officers didn't make much of it. They helped the flow of information between the Senate and the navy, they arranged official trips abroad for senators, and they often accompanied them on those trips.

But John McCain had higher expectations, because his father had been the navy's chief lobby-ist to Congress during John's Naval Academy years. John knew what weighty effects politicians could have on the military, and he knew how Jack McCain had taken advantage of his position to promote the navy's interests. Roberta McCain had helped her husband entertain many important senators and congressmen at their town house on Capitol Hill. Now McCain made friends with senators and saw how political work got done in Congress. He took advantage of his opportunities to travel and learn firsthand about various foreign countries.

Naturally friendly and fun-loving, McCain transformed his office in the Russell Senate Office Building into a popular gathering place for senators. Republicans and Democrats alike were welcome. Although McCain considered himself a confirmed Republican, he didn't necessarily follow his party's line, and he was able to respect different points of view. The close friends he made among the senators included Senator Gary Hart, a Democrat from Colorado, as well as Senator William Cohen (Republican, Maine), and Senator John Tower (Republican, Texas).

Senator Tower was a powerful figure in the Senate, the chairman of the important Armed Services Committee. Like McCain's father and grandfather, Tower had served in the navy during World War II. Tower respected McCain's intelligence and his intense interest in history and world affairs. More than that, he was fond of McCain as the son he'd never had, and Tower did his best to bring McCain along.

During the years after his return from Vietnam, John McCain survived and thrived in most areas of his life. Sadly, his marriage to Carol fell apart. By the spring of 1979, he and Carol had separated.

That summer John McCain was promoted to the rank of captain. But he was not content. He wanted a career to equal that of his father and grandfather, and there seemed to be no chance of that in the navy. Because of the permanent injuries to his arms, he would never be given an important sea command, the next step in a naval career. And without such a command, he'd never reach the rank of full admiral.

Besides, McCain felt more and more drawn to a career in politics. Since returning from Vietnam, he'd made many public appearances, and it was clear that he was an effective speaker. In his Senate liaison work, he'd seen how deeply politicians could affect the armed services—often, in McCain's opinion, without understanding all the consequences of their actions. McCain thought he could do a better job, and he was attracted to such a position of power.

Meanwhile, as he escorted a Senate delegation on a

trip to China in April 1979, John McCain had made a stopover in Hawaii. There, at a reception in Honolulu, he met a young woman named Cindy Hensley. McCain fell in love with her that first evening. Cindy, the daughter of a wealthy Arizona beer distributor, was beautiful and intelligent. McCain was forty-two at the time, and she was only twenty-five, but she was a mature, thoughtful person. Although Cindy could have gone into her family's business, or done nothing at all, she had chosen to teach children with disabilities.

John and Carol McCain were divorced in February 1980. That May, John and Cindy were married in her hometown, Phoenix. Two of McCain's friends from the Senate, Gary Hart and William Cohen, were in the wedding party.

Chapter 7

Big Changes

While John McCain was sorting out his personal life, big changes were taking place in American politics. In 1980 Ronald Reagan, former governor of California, ran for election against President Jimmy Carter. McCain had many reasons to favor Reagan, the Republican, over Carter, the Democrat.

For one thing, McCain felt that President Carter had been weak on defense. Furthermore, McCain and Reagan were friends, having met shortly after McCain's return from Vietnam. Governor Reagan admired McCain as a genuine war hero, and McCain admired Reagan as a politician who shared his conservative values.

McCain was delighted when Ronald Reagan won the election in November. But shortly after President Reagan's inauguration in January 1981, a personal sorrow struck John McCain. His father died of heart failure on March 22, 1981, at the age of seventy.

Jack McCain was buried with honors in Arlington National Cemetery. His final resting place was near the grave where John's grandfather had been buried thirty-six years before. Secretary of Defense Caspar Weinberger attended the funeral, as did many high-ranking navy officers.

So did First Lady Nancy Reagan, even though President Reagan was in the hospital after an assassination attempt a few days before. John McCain and his brother, Joseph, each gave a eulogy for their father. John ended by reciting "Requiem," the Robert Louis Stevenson poem that he and his father had both loved.

McCain was glad he'd had the chance, last year, to explain to his father that he was going to leave the navy. He was sorry to disappoint his father, who loved the navy so wholeheartedly. Jack McCain had hoped that one day John would become a full admiral, the first son and grandson of full admirals to achieve the same rank. Still, he was proud of John's navy career, and he'd understood why his son felt he had to leave now.

In Congress, McCain thought, he might be able to make an important contribution to his country. He consulted his friends Senators Bill Cohen and Gary Hart about how to launch a political career. They advised him to start by building a political base in Arizona, where he and Cindy had just moved.

Otherwise, they cautioned, McCain risked being called a "carpetbagger," an outsider who was moving into the district only for political gain. He needed to volunteer for civic duties, to work for the Republican Party, to become known to the voters, and to get to know the people who might work for him and donate money to a campaign. After some years of this preparation, perhaps he could run for a local office — maybe even the state legislature.

This was good advice, but John McCain was in a hurry. He was impatient, and he was past forty years old. He planned to jump over these first steps and begin by running for Congress.

John and Cindy McCain were now living in Phoenix, where Congressman John Jacob Rhodes, a fellow Republican, was the representative for the neighboring First Congressional District. In January 1982, when Rhodes announced his retirement, McCain saw his chance. He immediately bought a house in the First District, to qualify as a candidate there.

In March, McCain declared himself as a candidate

for Rhodes's seat in the House of Representatives. Since moving to Arizona, he had made some political connections through Cindy's family. Also, he and Cindy could afford to donate some money to his campaign. And from his work as navy liaison, he had connections with national politicians who might be helpful.

Senator John Tower of Texas was one of these, and he was generous with his help. Although there were three other Republicans running against McCain in the primary election, Tower endorsed him and persuaded some influential Arizona politicians to support him. Tower also raised money for McCain from Republicans in Texas.

As McCain's friends in the Senate had warned him, his opponents accused him of being a carpetbagger. McCain shut them up by answering that he'd never lived very long in *any* place—in fact, his longest residence in one city was his stint as a POW in Hanoi, Vietnam. Thus without seeming to brag or even to bring the subject up himself, John McCain reminded voters that he was a decorated war hero.

Personable and forceful, McCain gained the support of many wealthy donors as well as voters. One of the main contributors to his campaign for congressman was Charles Keating, a wealthy banker and a former navy pilot, like McCain. With a well-funded campaign, McCain could pay for professionally made TV advertisements, which further helped to get his name known.

McCain threw himself into an intense campaign, walking through neighborhood after neighborhood to knock on doors and introduce himself to the voters. In the months before the primary election, he wore out two pairs of shoes. Although the polls had predicted that he would come in third out of the four Republican candidates, he was convinced he would win.

On primary Election Day in September, John McCain was a bundle of nerves. There was nothing more he could do now to get votes, so he went to a movie—*Star Wars*. But he was too distracted to sit still.

That night, it was clear that McCain had won the primary to become the Republican candidate for the Arizona First Congressional District. That meant he would almost certainly win the general election, because Republicans greatly outnumbered Democrats in his district. Continuing his door-to-door campaign (and wearing out a third pair of shoes), John McCain won the general election in November by more than twice as many votes as his Democratic rival.

In January 1983 John McCain was sworn into

the US House of Representatives, and his political career was launched. Right away, he lobbied hard to get assigned to the House Interior Committee, which dealt with the internal affairs of the country. Those included water rights and land reclamation, so vital to the people he was representing, the citizens of his district. He knew he had a lot to learn about such matters.

One of McCain's assignments in the House was to chair the Republican Task Force on Indian Affairs. This was not considered a nationally important post, but it was important to Arizona. Arizona had the third-largest population of Native Americans, and one-fourth of its area was taken up by Native American reservations.

During his campaign, John McCain had promised to spend every weekend in his Arizona district. That was a big promise, since Washington, DC, was two thousand miles from Phoenix. Yet during his first year he did manage to fly home from Washington on Friday night and fly back Monday, forty-seven out of fifty-two weeks. During these weekends he met with the people in his district, gave speeches, and attended local events. He was taking Bill Cohen's and Gary Hart's advice about building a political base — only he was doing it *after* being elected.

John McCain might be only a new member of the lower house of Congress, but he had been studying history, as well as living it, for many years now. He had strong opinions about the big decisions made by politicians and military leaders. In most questions he approved of President Reagan's policies, voting for his tax cuts and supporting his hard line with the Soviet Union and intervention in Central America.

But when President Reagan decided to send US troops to Lebanon as peacekeepers, Congressman McCain voted against the action. "The longer we stay in Lebanon, the harder it will be for us to leave," he said on the floor of the House. He didn't want American soldiers committed to a foreign conflict without a clear mission, as they had been in Vietnam.

It was surprising for a junior congressman to vote against a popular measure, supported even by a majority of Democrats. This was the beginning of McCain's reputation as a "maverick" politician, one who follows his independent opinions. A few months later, in October 1983, a suicide bomber in Beirut blew himself up in a Marine barracks, killing 241 US soldiers. At that point, President Reagan withdrew the American troops.

The next year, 1984, Congressman McCain was

up for reelection. No Republicans opposed him in the primary, and again he easily won the general election. Added to his victory, the McCains were especially happy at the birth of their first child. Meghan was born on October 23.

Early in 1985 John McCain made a trip back to Vietnam. Eight years before, when McCain was still in the navy, President Jimmy Carter had asked him to join a delegation to Vietnam. The purpose of that trip was a first step toward resuming normal diplomatic relations. Then McCain had refused, because it was too soon after his long and painful captivity.

But this time he agreed to go. He had moved on in life, and the emotions connected with his imprisonment were not quite so raw. Besides, the purpose of this trip was to urge the Vietnamese to cooperate in returning the bodies of American soldiers who had died there. McCain had a great sympathy for the families of soldiers. Twelve years after the United States had left Vietnam, many families were still not sure what had happened to their loved ones.

In Hanoi, McCain was surprised and puzzled to see a new monument beside the lake where he had been shot down. It was a statue of an American POW, kneeling with his hands in the air. The inscription on the monument stated that it had been built in honor of the Vietnamese people's air defense heroes, who had shot down "the famous air pirate," John McCain himself.

As McCain viewed the monument, a large crowd of friendly Vietnamese gathered around. "Mah-cain, Mah-cain," they chanted. It seemed he was more famous in Vietnam than he was back home.

CBS-TV filmed the event for a special with Walter Cronkite, anchorman of the CBS Evening News, titled "Honor, Duty, and a War Called Vietnam." It included footage of McCain showing Cronkite around the prisons where he had been locked up. He even had tea with the Vietnamese in a room next to a cell where he had been tortured. It was hard for McCain to be in a place where he and his friends had suffered so much. But he handled the stress with his typical humor, asking his Vietnamese hosts not to shut him back inside.

The experience might be stressful for John McCain the ex-POW, but it was excellent publicity for McCain the politician. Hundreds of thousands of voters back in Arizona, as well as around the United States, watched the engrossing special program. The program reminded viewers of

John McCain's background as a war hero, and it informed them of the good work that Congressman McCain was doing now.

Back in 1982, when McCain decided to run for Congress, he'd intended all along that the House of Representatives would be only a first step in his political career. He had his eye on the Senate. As McCain knew well from his time as navy liaison to the Senate, senators had enormous power. The president could not make treaties with other countries or appoint important officials, such as ambassadors, cabinet officers, and Supreme Court justices, without the advice and consent of the Senate.

Senators serve for terms of six years, compared to the two-year terms of the House of Representatives. Each senator represents an entire state, not just a district. They have larger staffs than congressmen and sit on more committees in Congress. Unlike congressmen, senators have a reasonable chance of running for president—and some of those candidates, like Abraham Lincoln and John F. Kennedy, have been elected to the highest office.

Now the distinguished senator Barry Goldwater, first elected to the Senate from Arizona in 1952, was due to retire soon. John McCain aimed to follow him into "the world's most exclusive club," as the United States Senate has been called.

Senator Goldwater, independent, outspoken, and honest, was a politician whom McCain admired tremendously. Goldwater had been an army air corps pilot in World War II; he was deeply patriotic and had great respect for the military. A lifelong resident of Arizona, he had done more than anyone to build the Republican Party in Arizona and the rest of the West.

Running for president against Lyndon Johnson in 1964, Goldwater had been painted as a warmonger, and he lost the election. But as McCain knew, Goldwater had correctly pointed out that the United States had no clear mission in Vietnam. It was President Johnson who had widened the Vietnam War and, in McCain's opinion, mismanaged it.

Chapter 8

Senator McCain

Early in 1986 Barry Goldwater announced that after representing Arizona in the Senate for thirty years, he would not run again. Almost immediately afterward, John McCain announced his candidacy. By now he was a popular and well-known congressman, and no other Republicans stepped forward to oppose him for the nomination. McCain campaigned vigorously anyway, earning his nickname "the White Tornado" from the media. His political hero Senator Goldwater served as his campaign manager.

John McCain was expected to win the general election, since his Democratic opponent, Richard Kimball, had nowhere near McCain's name recognition or funding. However, Kimball was able to goad McCain into losing his temper: he accused him of being obligated to moneyed interests such as defense contractors, big corporations, and Realtors. That was a swipe at McCain's honor, the ideal way to get him furious.

McCain's campaign staff knew that Kimball hoped to get McCain so angry that he'd say something unwise, and they worked to calm him down. McCain shouted at them, "I don't have a temper!" In debates with Kimball that fall, he was just barely able to control himself. However, in November, McCain easily defeated his Democratic opponent. Waiting for Election Day to end, he continued his tradition of going to a movie — *Crocodile Dundee* this time.

While John McCain was enjoying his election triumph, a classmate from the Naval Academy was undergoing a humiliating ordeal. John Poindexter had been first in the class of 1958, while McCain had ranked fifth from the bottom. Poindexter had gone on to a distinguished career in the navy and the Department of Defense, achieving the rank of vice admiral.

During the Reagan administration, Poindexter had held the important position of national security adviser to the president. But in November 1986, the Reagan administration had to admit that Poindexter was involved in selling arms to Iran, an enemy of the United States. President Reagan appointed McCain's friend and mentor, the former senator John Tower, to lead an investigation into the affair.

John Poindexter was called up to testify before the House Armed Services Committee. McCain was still a member of the committee, since his first term in the Senate would not begin until January 1987. Speaking to Poindexter before the session, McCain urged his former classmate not to take the Fifth Amendment, which allows a witness to refuse to testify if he might incriminate himself by doing so. Witnesses who "pled the Fifth" were assumed to be doing so because they were guilty.

To McCain, it was a matter of upholding the honor of the navy. "You can't become the first admiral in the history of the United States Navy to plead the Fifth," he told Poindexter. But Poindexter could and did. Later, while the hearings were still going on, McCain told a TV interviewer that he thought his former classmate had made "a terrible mistake." Some Republicans felt that McCain was disloyal to the Reagan administration in making such a statement in public.

It came out during the investigation that with Poindexter's knowledge, the profits from selling the arms to Iran were used to fund the Contras, a militant faction fighting the leftist Sandinista government in

Nicaragua. Congress had passed legislation forbidding such funding, and this was a way to get around the law. Poindexter would be convicted in April 1990, but the conviction was reversed on appeal in 1991. In December 1992 the Supreme Court refused to reinstate the conviction.

At the beginning of 1987, John McCain was sworn into the United States Senate by Vice President George H. W. Bush. McCain's wife and two little children looked on proudly as he took the oath to "defend the Constitution of the United States against all enemies, foreign and domestic." (In May 1986, during his campaign for the Senate, Cindy had given birth to their first son, John Sidney McCain IV.)

Cindy and John had already decided that they would not move to the Washington, DC, area, as so many politicians and their families did. Cindy loved Arizona, and she was determined to bring up their children there. Cindy's parents lived in Phoenix, so the family would have the constant support of two grandparents. John would continue his routine of flying home to Phoenix every weekend. In spite of his many commitments to his constituents, he would try to reserve Sunday to spend with his family.

Senator McCain's office in the Russell Senate Office

Building was down the hall from his old office as navy liaison. He was pleased to think how far he'd come since those days, but he intended to make his new office, too, a social hub. McCain was glad to be appointed to the Committee on Commerce, Science, and Transportation, as well as the Select Committee on Indian Affairs. He was especially happy to have a seat on the Committee on Armed Services. Now *he* could be one of the senators who made decisions that so greatly affected the navy and other branches of the armed services.

Senator Robert Dole of Kansas, the Republican leader in the Senate, treated McCain with consideration and respect from the first. That meant a great deal to McCain, who admired Dole tremendously. Bob Dole was a decorated hero of World War II. He had almost died in combat, and his right arm was paralyzed as a result of his injuries.

The junior senator from Arizona seemed to be off to a good start. The next year, 1988, John and Cindy McCain's third child and second son, James Hensley McCain, was born in May. He was named after Cindy's father, James W. Hensley.

The year 1988 was also the fourth year of President Ronald Reagan's second term, and therefore his last year as president. Reagan's vice president, George H. W. Bush, was the natural Republican nominee for that year's election. During the campaign, John McCain was often discussed in the media as a possible vice presidential candidate, although he heard nothing from the Bush campaign about this. However, McCain was asked to give a speech on foreign policy and national defense, one of the main speeches, at the Republican convention in August.

In March 1988 McCain told a reporter that it was time for the United States to move toward a friendly relationship with the former enemy, Vietnam. His thinking about Vietnam had moved on since his prisoner-of-war years. But his memories of imprisonment were still vivid, and in his speech at the convention he told a story from those days.

One of McCain's fellow POWs, Mike Christian, had sewn himself a little American flag. Using a bamboo needle and bits of red and white cloth, he'd constructed the flag on the blue background of the inside of his shirt. Every day Christian would hang his shirt on the wall to display his flag, and McCain and all the other prisoners would recite the Pledge of Allegiance.

The Vietnamese found out about the flag, beat

Christian severely, and took away his shirt. But moments after Christian stumbled back into his cell, McCain said, he took up his needle. Although his eyes were swollen almost shut from his beating, he began sewing a new flag.

Everyone in the convention hall, including President Reagan, wept as they listened to McCain. Most people were astounded the next day when George H. W. Bush presented his running mate—not John McCain, but an unknown senator from Indiana, Dan Quayle. That November, Bush easily beat the Democratic candidate, Governor Michael Dukakis of Massachusetts.

In the first months of 1989, John McCain gained respect and fame with everything he did. First, he became known for a confirmation fight he led in the Senate. President Bush had nominated McCain's old friend and mentor from his navy liaison days, John Tower, for secretary of defense. But the Senate had to confirm the nomination, and Tower had made numerous political enemies during his career in the Senate. Also, the Democrats were still angry with President Bush for some of the tactics his campaign had used to defeat Michael Dukakis.

John McCain thought that Tower was the ideal

choice for secretary of defense. He was shocked and outraged to hear Tower attacked during the confirmation hearings before the Senate Committee on Armed Services. Worse, Tower's reputation was besmirched, as many witnesses came forward to state that he had a serious alcohol problem and also had harassed several women. These sensational accusations were leaked to the media, which played them up.

McCain did his best to dispute the charges and to persuade other senators to vote for Tower's confirmation. Defending his friend and former mentor from what McCain felt were false and unfair accusations, he lost his temper, shouting and swearing at other senators. But it was a losing battle. On March 9 President Bush gave up and withdrew Tower's nomination, substituting that of Richard Cheney.

John McCain was angry and sad that Tower was denied the Cabinet post, but McCain himself had benefited from the political fight. His defense of John Tower was written up in such influential newspapers as the *Washington Post* and the *New York Times*, and he appeared on the TV program *Meet the Press*. He was becoming well known.

Moving on after the Tower ordeal, Senator McCain worked on the goals he had promised to pursue when he was elected. For one thing, he wanted to limit "pork-barrel" spending. These were projects that legislators often tacked onto otherwise popular bills that they thought Congress and the president would probably pass. The pork-barrel items would please the voters in the legislators' home states, but wouldn't necessarily benefit the whole nation.

In April, McCain introduced a bill that would give the president the power to sign a bill, but veto a particular part of it that he disagreed with. He believed that this power, called the "line-item veto," would allow the president to cut vast amounts of "pork." However, others felt such a bill would give the president too much power, and it failed to pass.

John McCain also took an intense interest in Central America, where he saw political changes that could affect the United States. In both Nicaragua and El Salvador, leftist factions supported by the Soviet Union battled factions, such as the Contras, backed by the United States. In May 1989 McCain went to Panama, his birthplace, with a group of other senators to observe the national elections. The US delegation concluded that Manuel Noriega had rigged the election to win the presidency, and McCain felt that the United States should use military force to remove

Noriega from power. Later that year, the United States did invade Panama and remove Noriega.

McCain was riding high in October 1989, when a news story broke linking him to Charles Keating and Lincoln Savings and Loan. This was a scandal that had been brewing for some time. Charles Keating, a friend of John McCain's and a heavy contributor to his political campaigns, was the chairman of the board of the Lincoln Savings and Loan Association, owned by an Arizona corporation.

In March 1987 Keating came to McCain's Senate office and asked him to use his influence with the Federal Home Loan Bank Board, the government regulators who were investigating Lincoln Savings and Loan. McCain answered that it would be unethical for him to try to protect Keating from a legitimate investigation. Keating grew angry, accusing John of being a "wimp." That made McCain *very* angry. As far as he was concerned, that was the end of their friendship.

However, in April 1987 McCain did go to two meetings with Edwin Gray, the chairman of the Federal Home Loan Bank Board. Four other senators—Alan Cranston of California, Dennis DeConcini of Arizona, John Glenn of Ohio, and Donald Riegle of Michigan—also attended. All of them were concerned that Lincoln

Savings and Loan might be put out of business by overly harsh federal regulation.

At the second meeting, it came out that Keating had made risky investments with Lincoln Savings and Loan's deposits. In fact, its managers could actually be charged with criminal acts. At this point, John McCain was convinced that he should not defend Lincoln Savings and Loan. In his mind, he'd fulfilled whatever remaining obligation he had to his former friend Keating. He did not intend to be involved in the case any further.

But two years later Lincoln Savings and Loan went bankrupt, causing many retirees to lose their life's savings. In April 1989 the government had taken over the failed savings and loan association, as it was bound to do, since the deposits were federally insured. This move would cost taxpayers more than $3 billion. Now the question was, What role had John McCain, as well as four other senators, played in this disaster? Had they pressured the Federal Home Loan Bank Board not to regulate Lincoln Savings and Loan two years ago, when the cost to taxpayers would have been much less?

Lincoln was not the only savings and loan institution in trouble. There was a full-blown savings and loan crisis. During the Reagan years, federal regulation of S and L's had been loosened, and many of these institutions had made risky investments in commercial real estate. Congress, as well as the Reagan administration, had discouraged government agencies from supervising these activities.

The trouble for John McCain was, Charles Keating had not been only a friend—he had contributed heavily to McCain's political career since they'd first met in 1981. Altogether, Keating had raised $112,000 for McCain's campaigns for congressman and senator. McCain and his family had often accepted flights on Keating's private jet, worth more than $13,000, and they had neglected to pay for the flights.

Although Keating may not have expected or wanted payment for the flights, the ethics rules of the US House of Representatives required it. Also, McCain should have listed the flights as gifts in his annual financial statements. To make matters worse, Cindy McCain and her father had invested with Keating in an Arizona shopping mall. It looked as if Senator McCain, having accepted large financial favors from Keating, had felt obliged to shield him from investigation by federal regulators.

The Keating scandal ground on and on. In 1990

McCain's political enemies in Arizona organized a campaign to recall him. They did not succeed in collecting enough signatures to force a recall election, but it was a warning sign that many people in Arizona were disillusioned about Senator John McCain. He would be up for reelection in 1992, and he wondered if he could win. He feared that his political career, which had looked so bright only a few months before, might be doomed.

McCain, usually cheerful and energetic, became glum and quiet. His honor, so precious to him, had been blackened through his own carelessness. He knew that millions of Americans now believed he was the kind of politician who would do favors in return for gifts, and the idea made him miserable. Later he wrote that this time was "one of the worst experiences of my life." For a man who had endured years of imprisonment and torture, that was saying a lot.

In the fall of 1990, while Charles Keating was in jail, awaiting trial for fraud, the Senate Ethics Committee began holding hearings. Their purpose was to determine whether the "Keating Five," as Senators DeConcini, Riegle, Glenn, Cranston, and McCain were called in the media, had behaved improperly. All of the Keating Five except McCain were Democrats, and so the Democrats on the Ethics Committee weren't likely to go easy on McCain. They didn't want it to look as if Democrats were the only politicians who might have shifty ethics.

As John McCain gave testimony at the hearings, Cindy sat in the audience for moral support. John's mother, Roberta McCain, also attended the hearings, although she was recovering from a broken leg. McCain felt humiliated, not only from the blot on his honor, but also from wounded male pride. Over and over again he had to state, for everyone to hear, that Keating had called him a "wimp."

An added strain on the McCains was that Cindy was suffering from severe back pain. She had undergone back surgery in 1989, at the same time that the Keating scandal was becoming public, but the surgery didn't relieve her pain. Now she felt partly responsible for John's ordeal, since she was the one who paid the McCains' bills. She thought she'd already paid for the flights on Keating's jet, but she couldn't find the receipts.

After eight weeks of public hearings, televised on C-SPAN, the Senate Ethics Committee reported its findings at the end of February 1991. Although the five senators hadn't done anything criminal, they had delayed the investigation of Lincoln Savings and Loan, and thereby cost taxpayers $1 billion. Senator Cranston was found guilty of actual ethics violations, and Senators DeConcini and Riegle were guilty of the appearance of improper behavior. Senators Glenn and McCain, however, were guilty only of "poor judgment."

Even though John McCain had been cleared of any actual wrongdoing, he was deeply ashamed of his involvement in the scandal. Determined to clear his reputation, he gave the federal government $112,000, the total of the money that Keating had donated to his campaigns over the years. He also vowed to make campaign finance reform a main issue of his next election campaign.

Chapter 9

An Old War and a New War

The Keating scandal had taken a great deal of John McCain's time and attention, which he felt should have been spent on the nation's issues. In the meantime, a serious international crisis had exploded in the Middle East.

In August 1990 the dictator of Iraq, Saddam Hussein, invaded the neighboring country of Kuwait. He claimed that Kuwait was stealing oil from Iraqi wells, but to the rest of the world, the invasion was unprovoked aggression. Now his army was poised on the border between Kuwait and Saudi Arabia, and it seemed that he would invade that country next.

The United States, as well as most other nations, was outraged and alarmed. Saddam Hussein had not only waged unjust war—he was now threatening the world's supply of oil. If he took possession of Saudi

Arabia as well as Kuwait, he would control the majority of the oil reserves on the planet.

With the agreement of the United Nations, the United States and its allies demanded that Iraq withdraw from Kuwait by the beginning of 1991. When Saddam Hussein would not back down, President Bush asked Congress for permission to use US military force against Iraq. McCain spoke in favor of the request. "If we drag out this crisis and we don't at some time bring it to a successful resolution," he told the Senate, "we face a prospect of another Vietnam War." The Senate voted unanimously to authorize the president to use armed intervention in the Persian Gulf.

In January the United States and its allies began bombing Baghdad, the capital of Iraq. A few weeks later allied troops attacked Iraq. McCain continued to speak in support of the Gulf War, and he was frank about the importance of oil. "The world economy," he told an audience at Phoenix College, "is dependent on a free and unfettered flow of oil."

The war was over by the end of February, with the defeat of Iraq's army. After the fighting ended, McCain flew to Kuwait to observe the damage. It was a scene of utter destruction, since the Iraqi army had set fire to oil wells as they left Kuwait.

Senator John Kerry, with the same delegation to Kuwait, sat next to John McCain on the flight. They hadn't known each other well before this, since McCain was a conservative Republican from Arizona, while Kerry was a liberal Democrat from Massachusetts. John Kerry had also served in the navy during the Vietnam War, but Kerry had left the navy and organized veterans to protest the war. McCain, like other POWs, had been angry with all war protesters, including Kerry, for years after his release. But now that the two veterans and senators had the chance for a long talk, they found that they had a great deal in common.

To begin with, they respected each other's combat records. Unlike many war protesters, Kerry had volunteered for service in Vietnam and had been decorated for bravery in combat. Both men agreed that the United States should never have entered the Vietnam War, given that we had no clear goals. And they agreed that the war had been badly conducted and had been a horrific waste of lives and money.

Meanwhile, Cindy McCain was in Bangladesh that spring of 1991, with the American Voluntary Medical Team (AVMT). She had founded this nonprofit organization in 1988 to offer medical services to parts of the world where people were in desperate need. The AVMT arranged for medical workers to travel to areas of war or natural disasters to provide emergency care. Cindy herself led many of the trips.

On this trip to Bangladesh, she visited an orphanage run by Mother Teresa, the Roman Catholic nun awarded the Nobel Peace Prize for her work with the poor and helpless. Cindy noticed one particular Bangladeshi baby girl in the orphanage. The baby had a cleft palate so severe that without surgery, she would probably die. Cindy decided to bring this orphan back to the United States for medical treatment.

On the way home, Cindy McCain realized that she was going to adopt the baby. She hadn't had a chance to consult John, but she was confident that her husband would welcome this little girl into their family. When John met Cindy and the baby at the airport, he asked, "Where's she going?" "To our house," Cindy admitted. John laughed and said, "I thought so." The McCains named their new daughter Bridget.

While Cindy was on this tour with the AVMT, John McCain had been in Vietnam again, working for the POW-MIA cause. He had been appointed to a congressional committee, chaired by Senator John Kerry, with the goal of resolving the POW-MIA issue. Thousands of Americans were still in agony, waiting to learn the fate of the 1,665 servicemen missing in action (MIA) since the end of the Vietnam War.

It was nearly impossible that any of the MIA soldiers could be alive, although their families naturally hoped they were. The *Rambo* action movies, starring Sylvester Stallone, had given many people the false impression that the Vietnamese military was still holding POWs. Also, a photo of three men, supposedly American POWs in Southeast Asia, appeared on the cover of *Newsweek* and was widely circulated in the media. Although the picture proved to be a hoax, many friends and relatives of MIAs clung to the belief that their loved ones were still alive and in captivity.

Visiting Vietnam in April 1991, John McCain was suspicious of the motives of the Vietnamese government. But he got along well with their foreign minister, Nguyen Co Thach. He had long discussions with Thach, whom he respected for his intelligence and practical attitude. McCain could understand the Vietnamese point of view: Why did the United States expect them to produce information about 1,665 missing American soldiers, when *three hundred thousand* Vietnamese soldiers were still MIA? However, Vietnam did agree to open a POW-MIA office in Hanoi from which Americans could search for information.

In 1992 Senator John McCain was up for reelection. Without the Keating scandal, his victory would have been a sure thing, but now he had to overcome a tarnished reputation. The story of the Keating Five scandal was kept alive that year, as Charles Keating was convicted in state court and sentenced to ten years in prison.

Luckily, McCain's opponents for his senate seat were nowhere near as well known or as well backed as he was. Also, his reputation had revived somewhat during the Gulf War. As a former military man, his opinion about the war was respected, and he gave several speeches on the subject. Now Colin Powell, the chairman of the Joint Chiefs of Staff and immensely popular because of his role in winning the Gulf War, endorsed John McCain. So did Senator John Kerry, now a good friend of McCain's from their work together on the POW-MIA issue.

As John McCain campaigned for reelection as senator, George H. W. Bush campaigned for reelection as president. President Bush had been popular after the success of the Persian Gulf War, but by the beginning of 1992, most Americans were more concerned about the downturn in the US economy. Governor Bill Clinton of Arkansas, the Democratic nominee for president, took advantage of the change in national mood. With the slogan "It's the economy, stupid," Clinton's campaign managed to make President Bush seem unaware that ordinary Americans were struggling.

In November, Senator McCain won his reelection easily, but President Bush was defeated. This dampened McCain's joy in his own victory somewhat, because he believed that Bush was much better qualified than Clinton to be president. Also, McCain was critical of Bill Clinton for avoiding service during the Vietnam War.

During President George H. W. Bush's four years in office, John McCain had respected him for his tough stance on defense industry contracts. One program that Bush had tried to end was the Seawolf nuclear-powered attack submarine, to be built in Groton, Connecticut. McCain was all for military preparedness, but he felt that many defense contracts were nothing more than pork-barrel projects. McCain attacked the Seawolf program, pointing out that this sub had been designed as a weapon in the Cold War against the Soviet Union. Since the Cold War was now over, he argued, it was a huge waste of billions of taxpayer dollars.

In the end, the Seawolf program was limited to three submarines. And the senators from Connecticut, the defense contractors, and the Pentagon would be angry with John McCain for years afterward.

Chapter 10

Maverick

In January 1993, as President Bill Clinton began his first term, the congressional committee on the POW-MIA question turned in its final report. Their main conclusion was that "there is, at this time, no compelling evidence that proves that any American remains alive in captivity in Southeast Asia." All the committee members, whether they were Democrats or Republicans, hawks or doves, agreed.

John McCain and John Kerry also agreed that it was time for the United States to resume normal diplomatic relations with Vietnam. President Clinton wanted to move toward this goal, but it was politically difficult for him, because he had avoided serving in the Vietnam War. Senators McCain and Kerry, both decorated war veterans, gave Clinton the support he needed.

McCain and Kerry publicly lobbied to lift the trade embargo the United States had imposed on Vietnam nineteen years before. Early in 1994, they presented a resolution to the Senate allowing President Clinton to end the US trade embargo against Vietnam. This was an important step toward normalizing relations with the former enemy.

In May 1993 John McCain had been invited to the Naval Academy at Annapolis as the commencement speaker. In his speech he joked about his undistinguished academic record and the enormous number of demerits he'd racked up. He mentioned that his own father had been the commencement speaker in 1970—when McCain was still in prison in Hanoi.

Now McCain spoke passionately about what the navy meant to him. "For much of my life," he told the graduating midshipmen, "the navy was the only world I knew. It is still the world I know best and love most."

The Democrats held a majority in Congress in 1993, so President Clinton was optimistic about achieving his goals. One of his main goals was reforming national health care, especially to give all Americans medical insurance. He appointed a task force, headed by First Lady Hillary Clinton, to come up with an ambitious plan.

John McCain did not agree with Senate Republican leader Bob Dole that there was no crisis in health care. He thought there was a serious health care problem, and he agreed with the Clintons that all Americans ought to have health care. But he thought the plan the Clinton task force came up with was socialized medicine, in which the government pays for health care services.

Believing that such government interference would ruin the high-quality American health system, McCain was firmly opposed to it. Many other members of Congress, as well as the health insurance industry and the American Medical Association, also opposed the Clinton administration's health care reform. By September 1994, it was clear that the Clinton health care plan had failed.

Meanwhile, McCain was coping with a health care problem of his own. In December 1993 he underwent minor surgery to remove from his shoulder a malignant melanoma, a serious form of skin cancer. Melanoma can be deadly, but McCain, in his usual style, refused to be alarmed. He forged ahead with his busy schedule.

Later in December, he went to Russia with a bipartisan delegation, a group composed of both Republicans and Democrats. Vice President Al Gore was also in the delegation. The purpose of this trip was to monitor the Russian elections. These were the first free elections that had been held in Russia since the fall of the Soviet Union in 1991, and President Boris Yeltsin had asked the United States, with its long experience of elections, for help. It seemed like a triumph for democracy in the world, and it was an exciting assignment for John McCain.

In 1994 as McCain was working on the resolution to lift the Vietnam trade embargo, it came out that Cindy McCain had previously been dependent on painkilling drugs. She began taking the painkillers for severe back pain, but she ended her three-year dependency even before surgery in 1993 resolved her pain. Now, however, an Arizona newspaper published an article unflattering to Cindy about the episode. John was angry to see his wife attacked, and he defended her vigorously.

In July 1994 McCain experienced a proud moment in his family's tradition of service in the navy. He attended a ceremony at the Bath Iron Works in Bath, Maine, a shipbuilding center. Former president George H. W. Bush was to commission, to formally put into active service, a new destroyer. Its name was the

USS *John S. McCain*, honoring both Admiral John S. McCain Sr. and Admiral John S. McCain Jr. In his remarks, McCain said of his father and grandfather, "They were my first heroes, and their respect for me has been the most lasting ambition of my life."

While Cindy McCain was struggling with the publicity about her addiction, John was still sore from his involvement with the Keating Five. Although the Senate had acquitted McCain of any wrongdoing, the charges still rankled him. All his life, even at his wildest and most rebellious, he had thought of himself as a person of honor. He was ashamed that he had been publicly accused of dishonor, and he wanted to redeem his reputation.

Also, McCain was looking ahead to perhaps running for president. He felt that the next election, 1996, would be too soon, but 2000 was a distinct possibility. In a campaign for president, his opponents would jump on any weakness, fairly or not. McCain knew it would be important for him to overcome the black mark of the Keating Five.

He had thought long and hard about the Keating scandal. For one thing, it had made him realize how much politicians in Washington depended on large donations from special interests, the organized groups that seek to influence them. Political campaigns, especially campaigns for president, had become extremely expensive.

In the presidential primary races of 1976, Republican Gerald Ford's campaign had raised $13.5 million, while Democrat Jimmy Carter's campaign had raised $12.4 million. In 1992 Republican George H. W. Bush had raised $38 million, and Democrat Bill Clinton $37.6 million. Even allowing for the fact that the 1992 dollar wasn't worth as much as the 1976 dollar, this was an enormous jump. American voters were aware of the vast amounts of money required to run a presidential race, and it made them cynical about politicians and elections.

In the mid-1970s, after the Watergate scandal and President Nixon's resignation, there had been a mood in Washington to reform politics. In 1974 Congress had passed important amendments to the Federal Election Campaign Act of 1971 (FECA), which required that the figures for campaign contributions and spending be made public. The amendments also limited the amounts of money that could be contributed to campaigns and the amounts of money that could be spent. And FECA provided public funding, so that candidates didn't have to depend on private contributions.

For some years this law had worked well. However, the restrictions had been gradually loosened, until by the 1990s, they were meaningless. Determined to reform the system, McCain was especially concerned about the problem of "soft money." Under campaign finance laws, corporations or trade unions could not donate money directly to a candidate ("hard money").

The laws limited the amount that any one individual could give a candidate. However, donations to a political party, rather than to a candidate, were not nearly as strictly regulated. This "soft money" could then be used by the parties to help their candidates.

Also, any interest group could spend millions of dollars to run an "issue ad." Such advertisements could still contain obvious appeals to vote for or against a candidate, as long as the ad didn't say outright words such as "Vote for so-and-so" or "Don't vote for so-and-so." They were legally considered "free speech" rather than political advertising. They didn't even have to reveal who had paid to run the ad.

Looking for an ally to push for campaign finance reform, John McCain enlisted the help of a Democratic senator with a squeaky-clean reputation: Russell Feingold of Wisconsin. They developed a bill, which they introduced in the Senate in 1995. However, it went nowhere that year.

In July 1995 Senators John McCain and John Kerry stood beside President Clinton at a formal White House ceremony as he resumed diplomatic relations with Vietnam. Bill Clinton needed their political support for this act, especially now. In the midterm elections of 1994, the Republicans had seized control of both the House of Representatives and the Senate, for the first time since 1954.

Senator McCain was increasing his reputation as a maverick politician. "Maverick" in this sense is one who follows his own judgment, rather than necessarily voting with his party or even going along with the majority of his fellow senators. In backing normalization of US relations with Vietnam, McCain also further angered the families and friends of Vietnam soldiers still listed as missing in action.

These people were already disappointed with McCain for the report of the select committee on the MIAs. An unofficial veterans' publication, the *U.S. Veteran Dispatch*, accused McCain of collaborating with the communists in Vietnam. They also claimed that he had never been brutally tortured.

That summer *The Nightingale's Song*, a book by Robert Timberg about five graduates of the US Naval Academy, was published. It included a frank description of John McCain's years in Vietnam. Most reviews were full of praise for the book, but one reader was sternly critical of the part about McCain.

Roberta McCain called up her son and scolded, "Johnny, I'm going to come over there and wash your mouth out with soap." She was appalled to learn, for the first time, that he had shouted obscenities at his captors. Feebly McCain protested that they were "bad people." But to his mother, that was no excuse.

As for those who resisted normalizing relations with Vietnam, McCain believed in letting the Vietnam War end, especially since there were always new wars coming along to worry about. Another international crisis, in the Balkan Mountains in southeastern Europe, had been growing for years. Armed conflict between Bosnian Serbs, backed by Yugoslavia, and Bosnian Muslims had been raging since 1993.

At first McCain spoke against US involvement in the Balkans, but now it came out that the Serbs were engaging in what they called "ethnic cleansing," or getting rid of an undesired ethnic group by any means. This included the Serbs' horrendous slaughter of more than eight thousand unarmed Muslim men at Srebrenica. It was the worst mass murder in Europe since World War II.

In December 1995 Senator McCain and Senate Majority Leader Robert Dole cosponsored a resolution to allow President Clinton to send US troops to Bosnia. They also opposed a movement among Republicans to stop funding American troops in the Balkans. John McCain remembered how betrayed he'd felt, during his POW years in Vietnam, when he heard that Congress was trying to cut off funding for the military.

Making a speech to the Senate in favor of their resolution, Dole mentioned a fact that touched McCain deeply. It seemed that while McCain was a POW in Vietnam, Bob Dole had worn a bracelet with McCain's name on it. Although the two senators had been friends for years, this was the first McCain had heard of it.

In 1996 Bob Dole was one of the Republican candidates running for president. The Republicans were hopeful this year, since they had taken over both the House of Representatives and the Senate in the congressional elections of 1994. At first McCain backed Senator Phil Gramm of Texas, his closest

Senate friend at the time, and served as his campaign chairman.

Before the New Hampshire primary election in February 1996, Gramm dropped out of the race to support Bob Dole. McCain was then happy to endorse Dole, and a few months later it was clear that Dole would be the Republican nominee. That June, when Dole resigned from the Senate in order to focus on his campaign, McCain gave a moving speech. "We fought in different wars," the younger veteran said of Dole, "but we kept the same faith."

There seemed to be a strong possibility that Bob Dole might choose McCain for his running mate. Another possible Republican candidate for vice president was George W. Bush, governor of Texas and son of former president George H. W. Bush. Dole did choose John McCain to give the nominating speech at the Republican National Convention in August. But in the end, Dole picked former congressman and Housing and Urban Development (HUD) head Jack Kemp as his candidate for vice president.

Chapter 11

Straight Talk

One of Bob Dole's disadvantages, in running for president, was his age of seventy-three. He was the oldest first-time presidential nominee, older even than Ronald Reagan in 1980. Another disadvantage was that Dole came across in public as gloomy and reserved. In contrast, Bill Clinton, running for reelection, projected a young, cheerful, friendly image.

John McCain was aware of this problem. Accompanying Dole on the campaign trail, he did his best to make his friend appear more upbeat. Sometimes, sitting in the front row of the audience, McCain held up a hand-drawn smiley-face sign for Dole to see.

Another disadvantage for Bob Dole was that he'd had to wage a long primary campaign against Republican opponents. President Bill Clinton, on the other hand, had no Democratic challengers. He could concentrate on running his campaign for the general election months before Dole could, and he succeeded in portraying Dole as an elderly, out-of-touch conservative. President Clinton was reelected in November 1996 by a wide margin.

In March 1996 John McCain had been happy to see his anti-pork-barrel legislation, the line-item veto, finally pass Congress. He now had high hopes for the McCain-Feingold campaign finance reform bill, which he reintroduced that June. But during 1997, McCain-Feingold met fierce resistance in the Senate.

Senator Mitch McConnell of Kentucky denounced it as "an unconstitutional, undemocratic, bureaucratic boondoggle." Many senators were offended that John McCain, only a few years after the Keating scandal, was preaching to *them* about ethics. The bill was quickly killed.

Both political parties were alarmed that they might not raise nearly as much money if "soft money" was banned. Groups such as the National Rifle Association (NRA), a powerful lobby that opposed attempts to regulate firearms, were also against McCain-Feingold. If they couldn't furnish large sums to support particular politicians, their influence might be reduced. Of course, that was the idea of the bill, and the challenge only made McCain fight harder. He and his fellow reformer didn't give up.

During this time McCain was inspired in his drive for reform by reading biographies of Theodore Roosevelt. Roosevelt, president from 1901 to 1909, had always been a hero to McCain's grandfather and father, as well as to John himself from boyhood on. Before becoming William McKinley's vice president, Roosevelt had been assistant secretary of the navy. As president he wasn't afraid to use military force or to intervene in other countries, especially Latin America. He expanded the role of the United States in world affairs.

One quotation from Theodore Roosevelt especially seemed to express John McCain's ideal of the way all three generations of McCains had tried to live their lives: "All of us who give service, and stand ready for sacrifice, are the torch-bearers. We run with the torches until we fall, content if we can then pass them to the hands of other runners. . . . These are the torch-bearers; these are they who have dared the Great Adventure."

Like McCain, Roosevelt had radiated energy and enthusiasm. As a forceful leader, Roosevelt made many political enemies. But he accomplished important reforms, restraining the power of business monopolies. In 1907, under the Roosevelt administration, corporations had been barred from paying for advertisements for or against a candidate in a federal election.

In February 1998 the Senate voted down campaign finance reform again. John McCain had failed (so far) in his goal of passing this bill, but he'd gained national attention for trying. He had also made enemies of many lobbying groups and fellow politicians. For one thing, conservatives tended to see restrictions on political spending as a violation of free speech. Several groups in both parties were using soft money and issue ads to their benefit, and they didn't want to have to stop. Some senators thought that McCain was trying to make himself look good by making them look bad, and they resented it.

It was now less than two years until the opening of the presidential primary elections of 2000. In order to run a successful campaign for president, a candidate had to start planning years in advance. Many people suspected that John McCain was working toward a presidential bid, although he wouldn't discuss it publicly. When asked in August 1998 if he had any thoughts about becoming president, McCain joked, "I'd rather be emperor."

As if he hadn't made enough political enemies, during this time he added another: the powerful tobacco lobby. In his role since 1997 as chairman of the Senate Committee on Commerce, Science, and Transportation, he pushed a bill aimed at reducing teenage smoking by raising the tax on cigarettes. The Clinton White House also backed the bill, but most Republican senators opposed it. After a $50 million advertising campaign against the bill by the tobacco companies, it was killed in the Senate in June 1998.

During 1998, a growing scandal overshadowed the political scene in Washington and weakened President Bill Clinton's administration. It came out that President Clinton had committed perjury, or lied under oath, about his relationship with Monica Lewinsky, a White House intern. For lying under oath, the Republican-controlled House of Representatives impeached the president in December 1998. Impeachment meant that President Clinton would be tried by the Senate for improper conduct in office. If found guilty, he would be removed from office.

After a twenty-one-day impeachment trial, the Senate, acting as the jury, voted early in 1999. Some Republicans were eager to convict Clinton simply because he was a political enemy, and others because they were disgusted at his behavior. But John McCain had often supported the president, a Democrat, when he thought it was the right thing to do. Also, he did not think Clinton deserved to be removed from the presidency because of the way he conducted his personal life.

However, McCain believed that since the president's private life had become public, he was bound to tell the truth about it under oath. McCain therefore voted to convict. But most of the Senate voted to acquit, and President Clinton served the remaining two years of his second term.

Meanwhile, in November 1998 Senator McCain had won reelection in Arizona by a wide margin. That victory convinced him to run for president in 2000, and in April 1999 he announced his candidacy. In August 1999, as he was campaigning, he published a memoir about his family, his youth, and his years as a POW in Vietnam.

Faith of My Fathers, coauthored by McCain's chief of staff and speechwriter, Mark Salter, was enormously successful. It is common for a candidate for president to write an autobiography, in order to become better known to voters. However, most such campaign biographies are bland and unrevealing. True to his boisterous personality, John McCain's memoir was straightforward and punchy. It was a great read.

Incredibly, McCain's enemies again tried to spread rumors that he had not actually been tortured, as he claimed, in the Hanoi prisons. But there were too many witnesses to the truth of McCain's story: POWs who had been tortured during the same period as he was. Colonel Bud Day, one of McCain's first cellmates in Hanoi, and Everett Alvarez, the first American pilot to become a POW in Vietnam, appeared with McCain during the campaign and spoke to interviewers about just what it was like in the Hanoi Hilton.

John McCain didn't brag about his war record; in fact, he made jokes about it. "I would like to point out that it doesn't take a lot of talent to get shot down," he told his audiences. "I was able to intercept a surface-to-air missile with my own airplane."

McCain knew his candidacy was a long shot, because the Republican Party did not want to back him in his run for the White House. He'd offended too many big supporters of the party, including the tobacco lobby, the National Rifle Association, and the National Right to Life Committee. The party didn't like his bill for campaign finance reform either.

The campaign finance reform bill passed the

House of Representatives in September 1999, but it faced fierce opposition in the Senate. In October the Senate once again managed to kill the McCain-Feingold bill. However, John McCain still wasn't discouraged. In a way, the Senate's resistance only made his point about how soft money was corrupting American politics.

The favorite of the Republican Party, among the several candidates for president, was George W. Bush. Bush was governor of Texas, the second-largest state; he was favored by the Christian right, a powerful segment of the Republican Party; and he would have the advantage of the Bush family connections. And since he was a son of former president George H. W. Bush, George W. Bush's name was well known to voters.

To get John McCain's name better known, his team decided on a brilliant move. They would invite reporters onto McCain's campaign bus, named the "Straight Talk Express," and McCain would answer their questions frankly. This was quite different from the usual policy of presidential campaigns. Normally, campaign staff tried to limit the media's access and carefully control the candidates' public statements.

Reporters loved the Straight Talk Express. In

the front of the bus, McCain's aides worked tirelessly on cell phones and computers, directing the campaign. In the back section, McCain held center stage in a red leather swivel chair, talking with as many reporters as could squeeze on board the bus. He shared fast food with the reporters, traded jokes with them, and answered their questions frankly for hours on end. This approach paid off in a great deal of favorable publicity for presidential hopeful John McCain.

McCain also asked his mother to take part in his campaign. Although Roberta McCain had always taken a lively interest in politics, she was reluctant to be in the public eye herself. Besides, she was busy traveling around the world with her twin sister, Rowena, as she had done for years. But Roberta was still charming and attractive at the age of eighty-eight, and McCain thought it would help his cause if voters got to know her.

He also wanted Cindy to campaign with him, but he was afraid his opponents would attack him by publicizing her former prescription-drug dependency. Although Cindy's episode of drug dependency had come out in 1994, and it had become known in Arizona, it had not received that much national attention. Trying to forestall such attacks, in October 1999 John and Cindy McCain appeared on NBC-TV's *Dateline* and discussed her former dependency openly.

New Hampshire was a key state in presidential campaigns, because it held the earliest primary elections. Since the spring of 1999, John McCain had been campaigning in New Hampshire off and on. Now he and his team believed that he had a good chance of winning that state's Republican primary in February 2000. His independent, straight-talk style appealed to many New Hampshire voters, and so did his promises to reform campaign finance and protect Social Security.

At first, George W. Bush's campaign had felt confident about winning New Hampshire. Bush played up his plan for a large cut in taxes, which usually appeals to voters. But John McCain argued that Bush's tax cut would benefit wealthy Americans much more than it would those who needed tax relief. Worse, it would drain money from Social Security payments, which most Americans counted on for retirement. During January 2000, Bush's lead in the New Hampshire polls slipped steadily away.

To undercut John McCain's lead, the Bush

campaign spread the idea that he was unfit to be president because of his hot temper. They even hinted that the extreme stress of his captivity in Vietnam had made him emotionally unstable. To disprove this claim, McCain released his medical records to the press. Tests that McCain took immediately after his release in 1973 showed that he had returned from Vietnam more mature and stable than he had been before.

On February 1, 2000, John McCain received 49 percent of the Republican vote in New Hampshire, compared with George W. Bush's 31 percent. McCain's supporters (often called "McCainiacs") were over-joyed. This victory seemed to confirm McCain's belief that the voters really wanted straight talk.

McCain himself tried not to get too excited about his big win in New Hampshire. Back in Vietnam, he'd learned not to let his emotions be ruled by cir-cumstances he couldn't control. As he and the other POWs used to tell one another, "Steady strain."

Now McCain faced a big challenge in the next pri-mary, South Carolina. The early polls showed that he had a slight lead over Bush. He seemed to have the advantage because of his military background, which was greatly respected in that state.

But John McCain already had one big strike against him in South Carolina. The Confederate flag, a reminder of the Civil War, was still flying over the state capitol. Currently the National Association for the Advancement of Colored People (NAACP) was leading an attempt to get the flag taken down. But many white South Carolinians were fiercely opposed, viewing the Confederate flag as an expression of pride in their history.

When John McCain was asked his opinion, he first said the Confederate flag was offensive, "a symbol of racism and slavery." That was "straight talk"— but McCain's campaign workers were horrified. They urged him to "explain" his honest opinion away before it cost him the election. Reluctantly he read a statement that while he understood both sides of the issue, he viewed the Confederate flag as "a symbol of heritage."

South Carolina was an extremely conservative state, and John McCain often took independent positions. So George W. Bush's approach was to establish himself immediately as the more conservative candidate. In a speech at Bob Jones University, a well-known conservative religious institution, Bush called himself "conservative" several times, to make sure the message got through.

As the campaigning in South Carolina went on, Bush also presented himself as more fit than John McCain to become commander in chief of the armed forces, one of the roles of the president. This might seem laughable to anyone who considered that McCain was a decorated hero of the Vietnam War. George W. Bush, instead of serving in Vietnam, had enrolled in the Texas Air National Guard.

The Bush campaign even found a leader of a veterans' group willing to say that McCain was opposed to benefits for veterans suffering from Agent Orange and Gulf War syndrome. They also claimed that McCain's purpose on the congressional committee on MIAs was to prevent families from finding out what had happened to their soldiers missing in action in Southeast Asia. Neither of these claims was true. Still, they did influence voters.

McCain had made enemies of the tobacco companies, and tobacco was a major crop in South Carolina. Now the National Smokers Alliance, a group supported by the tobacco industry, struck back. They ran an ad claiming that Senator McCain had sponsored a bill calling for an enormous tax increase. "Tax increase" was a surefire way to alarm voters, and the ad didn't explain that the increase had been a tax only on cigarettes. Or that it aimed to make it harder for teenagers to start smoking.

A main focus of John McCain's campaign — of his last several years, in fact — was his work for campaign finance reform, to rein in the enormous amounts of money spent to influence elections. Now George W. Bush declared that *he* was a reformer — a "reformer with results," as governor of Texas. Hearing this, McCain remarked sarcastically, "I understand Governor Bush is now a reformer. If so, it's his first day on the job." Bush's campaign, making good use of soft money, had raised more funds than any other candidate in the history of the country.

Chapter 12

"The Dirtiest Campaign"

Attack ads now flew back and forth across South Carolina. McCain's ads accused George W. Bush of "twisting the truth like Clinton." Bush complained that this was "about as low a blow as you can give in a Republican primary," and many voters seemed to agree with him. They had such a negative opinion of Bill Clinton that they thought it was unfair for McCain to link Bush with the disgraced president.

Several influential conservative Christian leaders, including Pat Robertson and Jerry Falwell, spoke out against McCain, suggesting that he wanted to limit religious freedom. Other Bush supporters sent out a flood of phone calls and e-mails suggesting that McCain was a traitor for encouraging US diplomatic relations with Vietnam. John McCain was used to the rough-and-tumble of political campaigns, but he was shaken by the nastiness of some of these attacks.

McCain finally decided to pull his own attack ads, and he asked Bush to do the same. Bush refused, and right up to Election Day in South Carolina, he kept accusing McCain of using negative ads against him. Mixing up his words, as he often did, Bush declared, "You can't take the high horse and then claim the low road."

The worst example of the "low road," in John McCain's opinion, was an attack on his wife. Toward the end of the South Carolina primary campaign, flyers and phone calls went out that accused Cindy McCain of being a drug addict. Cindy had stopped taking opiate painkillers in 1992, admitted her former dependency publicly in 1994, and explained it on national TV in 1999. But those facts didn't stop the malicious rumors from flying.

Other rumors, designed to appeal to racial bias in South Carolina, drew attention to Bridget, the McCains' adopted dark-skinned Bangladeshi daughter. At the attacks on his family, John McCain did lose his temper. He called the conservative Christian leaders Pat Robertson and Jerry Falwell "agents of intolerance."

On February 19 George W. Bush won the South Carolina Republican primary by a wide margin. This was a serious setback, but the McCain campaign went on fighting. "My friends," he told a crowd of "McCainiacs" in Michigan the very next day, "I lived in a hotel once where there were no mints on the pillow. I know how to take a punch, and I know how to fight back." The "hotel" he referred to, as his cheering audience knew, was the Hanoi Hilton, where he had survived years of starvation, filth, and torture.

All during the campaign of 2000, the "issue ads" that Senator McCain had tried to ban, along with "soft money," had an important influence. Before the Michigan primary on February 22, the Sierra Club (an environmental group) ran TV ads in Michigan showing disturbing pictures of air and water pollution in Texas. As the ad didn't have to say, Texas's governor was George W. Bush. McCain won the Michigan primary election.

After winning in Michigan and Arizona, John McCain felt hopeful about his prospects for Super Tuesday, March 7. On that date, Republican primaries would be held in thirteen states (and American Samoa). But first there were primaries in Virginia and Washington State, and George W. Bush won both of those.

The Bush campaign continued to come up with new, inventive attacks on McCain. One barrage of TV ads accused McCain of opposing funding for breast cancer research. This was ridiculous on the face of it, since McCain's own sister, Sandy McCain Morgan, was a breast cancer survivor. When he protested that he did support breast cancer research, Bush accused McCain of running an "angry campaign." The implication was that maybe McCain *was* too hot-tempered to be president.

John McCain did get angry enough to call Pat Robertson and Jerry Falwell an "evil influence" on the Republican Party. Reporters heard him say this on the Straight Talk Express, and the quote was quickly picked up and repeated by the national media. Since the Christian right leaders Robertson and Falwell were respected and admired by conservative Republicans, this "straight talk" cost McCain votes.

In Ohio, one of the most important Super Tuesday states, supporters of Bush fought back against the earlier Sierra Club ad showing pollution in Governor Bush's Texas. Their TV ad told voters, "Last year, John McCain voted against solar and renewable energy. That means more use of coal-burning plants that pollute our air. Ohio Republicans care about clean air. So does Governor Bush. . . ." In fact, Governor Bush had worked to keep Texas coal-burning plants from having to comply with the Clean Air Act.

On Super Tuesday, Bush won nine out of thirteen states, including the key states of Ohio, California, and New York. Two days later, John McCain announced that he was dropping out of the presidential race. One retired Democratic politician from South Carolina remarked that this had been "the dirtiest, nastiest campaign I've ever seen."

John McCain had to agree. What bothered him almost more than anything else, though, was his own dishonest statement about the Confederate flag controversy. A few weeks after leaving the race, he returned to South Carolina to confess. "I was raised to know that I should never sacrifice principle for personal ambition," he told the audience. "I regret very much having done so." McCain was criticized harshly by people on both sides of the issue, but his conscience felt better.

Some people now wondered if McCain might be a possible candidate for George W. Bush's vice president. But he firmly announced, even before the elections results came out, that he was not. "I can serve the country and my family much better by being the senator from Arizona," he told interviewers.

For some time after Super Tuesday, McCain avoided actually endorsing Bush. But the Republican Party, especially the Bush supporters, was determined to get McCain's endorsement. As the Republicans geared up to battle Vice President Al Gore, the Democratic nominee, it looked to be a close race. It was vitally important for the party to be united.

Finally a private meeting for Bush and McCain, followed by a press conference, took place on May 9 in Pittsburgh. McCain did endorse Bush's candidacy, but he did so in a joking way. "I endorse Governor Bush, I endorse Governor Bush, I endorse Governor Bush, I endorse Governor Bush, I endorse Governor Bush, I endorse Governor Bush," he chanted for the reporters. A photographer caught him grimacing as he stood beside Bush.

However, in the first part of August, at the Republican National Convention, John McCain gave a serious speech to help work up enthusiasm for his rival's candidacy. He also made several campaign appearances for George W. Bush after the convention. This was an effort, especially after McCain discovered on August 10 that he faced a personal health crisis. A biopsy of skin samples from his left arm and left temple had revealed that he had spots of malignant melanoma again.

On August 19 McCain underwent extensive surgery to remove the melanoma and the lymph nodes in his face and neck. He took some weeks off after the surgery, and he recovered well. But for the rest of his life, his left jaw would be slightly larger than his right jaw.

By October, McCain seemed as feisty as ever, in spite of the bruising political campaign and his medical problems. He appeared in TV ads to promote laws in Oregon and Colorado to close the "gun show loophole." In those states and many others, buyers at a gun show were not required to have background checks before purchasing a weapon. By opposing the gun show loophole, McCain further angered the National Rifle Association. They were already unhappy with him for his crusade for campaign finance reform.

In November 2000 the presidential election results were extremely close, too close to call. There had to be recounts in some states, especially Florida. Finally, there were questions about the Florida recount itself. The election was not settled until December 4, four weeks after Election Day, in George W. Bush's favor.

Although John McCain had lost the Republican primary election, campaigning had given him a national reputation and a better understanding of how to get things done in the Senate. Even before President George W. Bush's inauguration on January 20, 2001, Senator McCain plunged back into his favorite project: campaign finance reform. Reform seemed to be needed more than ever—during the presidential campaign of 2000, the candidates had spent a total of $343.1 million, about $100 million more than in 1996.

Senators McCain and Feingold planned to reintroduce their bill to the Senate on January 22. With the Senate evenly balanced between fifty Republicans and fifty Democrats, it seemed like a good time to get the parties to agree on the issue.

But President Bush and other Republican leaders tried to get McCain to hold off on campaign finance reform. First they wanted to enact the large tax cuts Bush had proposed during the election campaign. However, McCain didn't even approve of Bush's proposal for tax cuts, and he refused to wait. He introduced his bill and worked steadily to get it passed. Early in April, McCain-Feingold did pass the Senate, although it still faced a stiff battle in the House of Representatives.

The White House was already unhappy about what it saw as McCain's disloyalty. Then in June, the even balance between the parties in the Senate was upset.

Senator James Jeffords of Vermont decided to leave the Republican Party and become an Independent. That meant that the Democrats now controlled the Senate. Senator Tom Daschle, Democrat of South Dakota and a good friend of John McCain's, was majority leader.

Rumors flew that McCain would also leave the Republican Party, although he denied this. "I am a proud Republican and I hope we can maintain the tradition of Teddy Roosevelt and Barry Goldwater," he said.

Political observers called the lack of cooperation between President Bush and Senator McCain a "feud." On June 7 McCain voted against Bush's extensive tax cuts, the center of his administration's program. Of course, McCain wasn't just being ornery; he'd said Bush's tax cuts were a bad idea when Bush first proposed them during the 2000 campaign. He repeated that the Bush tax cuts didn't give the break to the people who needed it—lower- and middle-class Americans.

In Arizona, a new effort to recall Senator McCain sprang up. A small but passionate group of Arizona Republicans felt that John McCain did not really represent their party. He was too friendly with Democrats, he'd voted against the Bush tax cuts, and he was leading the charge for campaign finance reform, which seemed more likely to hurt Republicans than Democrats. This recall, like the one in 1990, didn't succeed, but it expressed the feelings of many party loyalists in Arizona and other states.

On the morning of Tuesday, September 11, 2001, Americans were stunned and terrified by a series of surprise attacks. John McCain was driving to the Senate Office Building in Washington when he heard the first news: a plane had hit the North Tower of the World Trade Center in New York. That might have been an accident—but at the office, he and his staff watched on TV as a second plane hit the South Tower. McCain told them, "This is war."

Later a Middle Eastern terrorist group called Al-Qaeda claimed responsibility for the carefully planned attacks. They had used hijacked planes to destroy the Twin Towers in New York City and damage the Pentagon, the headquarters of the US Department of Defense. A fourth, failed attempt was probably intended to hit the Capitol Building in Washington, DC. Three thousand people died, and six thousand more were injured. It was the worst foreign attack on American soil since Pearl Harbor in 1941.

That day, and for the next few days, Americans were terrified and bewildered almost to panic. President Bush could not reassure the nation immediately, since the Secret Service was flying him from one air force base to another to keep him safe. Many news organizations called John McCain, asking for his comments on the disaster. "The best thing that we can do as Americans is to remain calm," he said. In level, encouraging tones he told the people that their government was still running, and the president would return to Washington.

McCain had no doubt that the United States should respond to the attack with military force. He supported President Bush's declaration of a "war on terror" and his decision to attack the terrorist group Al-Qaeda. The counterattack would be launched in Afghanistan, where the Taliban, the reactionary Muslim government, was shielding Al-Qaeda leader Osama bin Laden. However, McCain felt that Bush should have immediately ordered an investigation of how the September 11 disaster had come about, as President Franklin Roosevelt had after Pearl Harbor in 1941.

In spite of the trauma of the September 11 attacks and the changed mood of the country, McCain kept working toward his goal of campaign finance reform. He was triumphant when the House of Representatives' campaign finance reform bill passed by a comfortable margin on February 14, 2002. On March 20 the Senate accepted the House bill and sent it to President Bush. John McCain had been looking forward to this moment for seven years.

President Bush felt that he had to sign the bill into law, rather than veto it. Since campaign finance reform was a popular idea with voters, he didn't want to seem to be against it. However, he signed it in just as grudging a way as McCain had endorsed Bush for president in 2000. Instead of holding a public signing with the media present, and with Senators McCain and Feingold honored as the bill's sponsors, President Bush signed the Bipartisan Campaign Reform Act quietly, with only a few witnesses from his own staff.

That September John McCain published a new memoir, *Worth the Fighting For*. This book picked up the story of his life after his release from prison in 1973 and ended in the spring of 2002 with the passage of McCain-Feingold. McCain promoted his new book on many radio and TV programs, including the popular TV comedy show *Saturday Night Live*.

Meanwhile, President Bush and his advisers were

preoccupied with the Middle East, especially Iraq. Iraq's ruler, Saddam Hussein, had threatened the stability of the region ever since his invasion of Kuwait in 1990. Now it was feared that Hussein was stockpiling weapons of mass destruction, such as chemical, biological, or nuclear weapons. In October 2002 the US Congress passed a joint resolution authorizing President Bush to use "any means necessary" to prevent Iraq from attacking the United States or its allies. John McCain strongly supported the resolution, stating that Iraq was "a clear and present danger to the United States of America."

Toward the end of 2002 Saddam Hussein unwillingly allowed United Nations inspectors to search for weapons in Iraq, and the inspection team did not find evidence of weapons of mass destruction. But the Bush administration insisted that they had evidence of Iraq's weapons of mass destruction, and also that Iraq was an ally of Al-Qaeda in its attacks on the United States. On March 20, 2003, the United States and its allies launched an invasion of Iraq.

Although John McCain supported the invasion, he criticized the way the Bush administration conducted the war. It reminded him of the Vietnam War, when American troops had been sent to fight without clear goals or a plan for following up the invasion. McCain also thought that Bush was wrong to push for more tax cuts during a time of war.

War, as McCain knew well from his work on the Senate Armed Services Committee, was hugely expensive. In May 2003 he voted against Bush's second round of tax cuts. And that November, after visiting Iraq, he criticized the way Secretary of Defense Donald Rumsfeld was running the war. McCain thought more troops were needed.

Even for someone who loved a good fight, John McCain was taking on several big issues. But another issue was looming, a global danger that threatened to dwarf all the others. For some years, scientists in the United States as well as other countries had warned that human activity was causing serious changes in the earth's climate. Burning fossil fuels, such as oil and coal, had produced so much carbon dioxide, a "greenhouse gas," that the global temperature was rising. A warmer global climate could result in crop failures, wildfires, increasingly violent hurricanes, and rising sea levels.

John McCain felt that the United States, as a major source of greenhouse gases, had a responsibility to reduce its emissions. He believed the best opportunity for doing so, without harming the economy, was a "cap and trade" plan. Working with Senator Joseph Lieberman, Democrat of Connecticut, McCain presented to the Senate the 2003 Climate Stewardship Act.

McCain and Lieberman's cap and trade proposal offered an economic incentive for businesses to limit their emissions. They believed that this approach would be more successful than simply ordering businesses to reduce polluting gases. However, the McCain-Lieberman bill was defeated in the Senate. John McCain and Joe Lieberman would try their version of "climate stewardship" two more times, in 2005 and 2007—with no success.

The year 2004 brought another presidential campaign, with President George W. Bush running for reelection. The Bush administration was afraid that John McCain was planning another run at the presidency. McCain denied this, but presidential hopefuls are often careful not to announce their plans too early.

John McCain, turning sixty-eight in 2004, seemed as energetic and forward-looking as ever. He compared his philosophy of life to Theodore Roosevelt's, who liked to go "full-bore," as Roosevelt put it. McCain's daughter Meghan remarked, "I know he had me later on in life, but I've never felt it." All McCain's children thought their father was fun to be around, and the national media agreed. Quick, witty, and outspoken, he was a favorite on TV programs such as *The Daily Show*.

In the end, Senator McCain did not run for president in 2004. Instead he went on a tour to promote another new book, *Why Courage Matters: The Way to a Braver Life*. In April, when Cindy McCain suffered a brain hemorrhage, McCain flew home to Phoenix to be with her.

John Kerry was the Democratic nominee for president, and there were rumors that McCain might run on the Democratic ticket as Kerry's vice president. McCain reminded them that he was a Republican. Still, he defended Kerry when a group of Bush supporters accused Kerry of lying about his injuries in Vietnam. They claimed that Kerry didn't deserve the Purple Heart, or the other medals he'd received for courage under fire.

McCain recognized this smear of Kerry's war record as the same kind of attack he'd suffered from Bush supporters in the campaign of 2000. He said pointedly, "I think John Kerry served honorably in Vietnam. I think George Bush served honorably in the Texas Air National Guard during the Vietnam War." However, in August 2004 McCain finally spoke at the Republican National Convention in support of President Bush, praising his "War on Terror."

Unlike many of the politicians who had urged President Bush to use military force, John McCain's support went deeper than talk. He himself had risked his life in military service, and his oldest son, Doug, had served as a navy pilot. Now his son John Sidney McCain IV was about to continue the family tradition by entering the Naval Academy.

In November 2004 President George W. Bush was reelected by a narrow margin. But John McCain won reelection to his Senate seat by 77 percent of the vote. At a time when the American public held a generally low opinion of politicians, McCain had the highest rating of any US politician.

Chapter 13

Defeat with Honor

As President George W. Bush campaigned for reelection, the wars in Afghanistan and Iraq had dragged on. And troubling stories surfaced about the US treatment of prisoners. In April 2004 the TV newsmagazine *60 Minutes* ran a story about prisoner abuse at Abu Ghraib, a US military prison near Baghdad.

The United States, like most of the countries of the world, had agreed to the United Nations Convention Against Torture of 1984. In spite of this, US military guards at Abu Ghraib humiliated and tortured prisoners, and there was some evidence that officials at the higher levels of the government had encouraged the abuses. Abu Ghraib became an international scandal, damaging US standing among the nations of the world.

Likewise there were accusations of prisoner abuse

at Guantánamo Bay detention camp, the military prison at the US naval base in Cuba. In 2004 the International Red Cross protested that the US military had constructed "an intentional system of cruel, unusual, and degrading treatment" for prisoners held at Guantánamo. Americans were shocked to learn that interrogation techniques approved by their government included "waterboarding," or simulated drowning.

Having been an abused prisoner of war himself, John McCain was deeply troubled by these reports that Americans were mistreating their prisoners. In October 2005 he introduced the McCain Detainee Amendment, an add-on to the House of Representatives Defense Appropriations Bill of 2005. This amendment prohibited inhumane treatment of prisoners, and it limited interrogators to the techniques listed in the US Army Field Manual. The McCain Detainee Amendment Act was passed by an overwhelming majority of the Senate and signed by President Bush. However, the president stated that he would not feel bound by this law if he thought that "protecting the American people from further terrorist attacks" was at stake.

Also in 2005, John McCain published another book, *Character Is Destiny*. Like the one before it, *Why Courage Matters*, this book was a collection of true stories about people he admired. Each one of them, from Mahatma Gandhi to Dwight D. Eisenhower, had remained true to his or her conscience, in spite of severe challenges.

One chapter told a story from McCain's POW years. The hero was a Vietnamese guard who had risked punishment just to show sympathy for a wretched American prisoner. One Christmas Day, as John McCain was enjoying his five minutes of standing outside his cell in the prison courtyard, this guard came up and stood beside him. He didn't look at McCain, but he silently drew a cross in the dirt, and they looked at it together.

That same year, 2005, on Memorial Day, the A&E Network aired a dramatization of John McCain's first book, *Faith of My Fathers*. McCain, visiting the movie set in New Orleans, was very impressed with Shawn Hatosy, the actor who played his young self. McCain also complimented the filmmakers on their recreation of Hoa Lo Prison in an old beer brewery—it was almost too realistic, he joked.

As a senator from Arizona, one of the four states that bordered Mexico, John McCain was naturally concerned with the problem of immigration. And increasingly, Americans in general were worried about the number of people coming from other countries to live in the United States. By 2006, it was estimated that about eleven million immigrants now lived and worked in the United States without legal permission.

After the attacks by Al-Qaeda on September 11, 2001, many Americans feared that it was too easy for foreign terrorists to enter the United States. Some Americans were also concerned that undocumented immigrants were taking jobs away from legal residents and overburdening public services such as schools and hospitals. On the other hand, many American agricultural businesses depended on these same immigrants for cheap labor.

Working with Democratic senator Edward Kennedy of Massachusetts, John McCain cosponsored the Secure America and Orderly Immigration Act, introduced in the Senate in May 2005. The bill proposed a realistic way to deal with the immigrants. At the same time, it tried to reassure Americans that the federal government could control the borders and that US citizenship must be fairly earned.

The McCain-Kennedy bill became the basis of the Comprehensive Immigration Reform Act of 2006, which passed the Senate but died in the House. However, many conservative Republicans were angry with McCain for sponsoring this legislation. They regarded the McCain-Kennedy bill as "amnesty," or too-easy acceptance of undocumented immigrants.

During President George W. Bush's second term, John McCain considered running for president again in 2008. Several years before, when an interviewer asked him about the possibility of running in 2004, McCain had said he couldn't envision it. "I'd be sixty-eight if I ran again." Now, if elected in 2008, he'd be *seventy-two* when he took office in 2009. He'd break the record set by his role model President Ronald Reagan, who was inaugurated at the age of nearly seventy.

But McCain's age didn't seem to slow him down. He was still the "White Tornado," wearing out his children, his Senate staff, and the reporters who tried to keep up with him. Also, he had a great deal going for him as a presidential candidate. He had a long and honorable record in the Senate. He was nationally known and had a high favorable rating among voters. He was respected for his military service, and for the fact that three of his children had served or were serving in the military.

In deciding whether to run in 2008, McCain discussed the question with Cindy and his children. A presidential campaign shone a harsh spotlight on a candidate's family, as the McCains knew well from the campaign of 2000. Cindy wasn't as concerned for herself as she was for Bridget.

Bridget, now sixteen, had just recently checked listings of her name on the Internet and discovered nasty rumors spread about her during the South Carolina primary in 2000. She had been shocked and upset. Before deciding to agree to this new campaign, Bridget met with her father's staff and questioned them closely about what she could expect this time.

In January 2007 President Bush announced that he was sending twenty thousand additional US troops to Iraq. John McCain applauded this move — he'd said from the beginning, in 2003, that the United States needed to commit more troops in order to win the war. But the "troop surge" was not popular with most Americans, who wanted the United States to get out of Iraq. Thousands of American soldiers had lost their lives, and thousands more had been disabled. As of 2006, the war had cost United States taxpayers over $200 billion.

In April 2007 John McCain formally announced

that he would be a candidate for president in 2008. This time, he decided, he would not run as the "maverick" he was often called. He wanted to be the clear choice of the Republican Party, and for that, he had to make amends with the conservative Republicans. He'd already begun to do this—in May 2006 he had spoken at the graduation ceremony at Jerry Falwell's Liberty University in Lynchburg, Virginia. Some of McCain's admirers were horrified that he would reconcile with conservative Christian leader Falwell, whom he'd called "an agent of intolerance" during the 2000 campaign.

At the beginning of 2007 McCain seemed to be the clear frontrunner, and his campaign presented him as the obvious choice for the Republican nomination. But as the year went on, McCain's campaign almost broke down over the issue of immigration.

Although the Great Recession would not officially begin until the end of the year, Americans already felt squeezed by economic hard times. The prices of private homes, which had been rising steadily for a number of years, finally collapsed. Homeowners who had taken out large mortgages, expecting their houses to increase in value, were left with property worth less than the loans they had to pay back. Many of them refused to pay or simply could not pay.

Hundreds of thousands of families faced losing their homes through foreclosure. To make matters worse, many mortgage lenders had sold the risky loans to investors, who now held worthless stock. The stock market dropped.

In this climate, Americans were even less willing than before to share jobs, schools, or hospitals with undocumented immigrants. A large number of Republican voters passionately opposed the Comprehensive Immigration Reform Act of 2007, which Senator McCain supported. Although President Bush also supported the bill, and although it provided increased border security over the Comprehensive Immigration Reform Act of 2006, it was so strongly resisted in Congress that it was dead by June. Meanwhile, McCain's position on immigration cost him money and backers. His campaign faltered.

Luckily for McCain, coming from behind always energized him, and he decided to turn his lack of funds into an advantage. In spite of the Campaign Finance Reform Act of 2002, the cost of presidential campaigns had continued to rise. In 2004 George W. Bush's campaign raised $258.9 million, while John Kerry's campaign had raised almost as much, $254.8 million. Some political observers predicted that each major candidate in the 2008 election would have to raise over $400 million.

This ballooning overspending outraged John McCain, and in the summer of 2007 he reorganized his campaign to cut expenses. He spent the second half of 2007 campaigning as an underdog candidate on his bus, the Straight Talk Express. By the time the primary elections began in January 2008, he had risen in the polls again.

Politicians' families can help a great deal in a campaign, giving the candidate an image as a likable family man. John McCain knew that his mother and Cindy would campaign for him, but he didn't want to pressure his children to step into the political spotlight. Most of the McCain children chose to stay backstage.

But Meghan McCain, now in her early twenties, joined in enthusiastically. She maintained a lively personal blog on the Internet about her experiences on the campaign trail. She posted pictures of herself with her family and friends, as well as some candid footage of her father—one clip showed him clowning as he turned ribs on the backyard grill.

John McCain's son Jimmy had joined the Marines at the age of seventeen, and he was now serving in Iraq. McCain was proud of his son, but he barely mentioned him as he campaigned. For one thing, he didn't want to exploit his son for political advantage. More important, he was concerned about Jimmy's safety. He remembered all too well how pleased the Vietnamese had been to capture him, the son of a famous admiral.

Roberta McCain made several campaign appearances, radiating her usual energy and charm. McCain called her his "secret weapon," joking that he scheduled joint appearances with her to prove to voters that he had good genes. Look how hale and hearty his mother was, at the age of ninety-six! He also threatened that if anyone said he was too old to be president, he'd have his mother go wash his or her mouth out with soap.

In January John McCain won the Republican primaries in New Hampshire, South Carolina, and Florida. In the Super Tuesday primaries on February 5, he won a majority of the states and delegates. On March 4, after winning primaries in Texas, Ohio, Vermont, and Rhode Island, he was informally acknowledged to be the Republican nominee, although it wouldn't be official until the Republican National Convention.

Now McCain faced a major challenge. Since he was the Republican nominee, voters would tend to associate him with the Bush administration. And in April 2008, President Bush's approval rating sank to 28 percent, one of the lowest ratings of any president in US history.

Americans were dismayed by the length and expense of the Iraq War, which by March 2008 had cost four thousand American lives and $600 billion from US taxpayers. Voters were especially unhappy with the severe slump in the US economy, which continued with no end in sight. To make life harder, the prices of gasoline and food had risen sharply since 2007.

In the Democratic Party primaries, the race had narrowed down to two contestants: former First Lady and now Senator Hillary Clinton of New York, and Senator Barack Obama of Illinois. While Senator Obama and Senator Clinton continued to fight for their nomination, John McCain went on a "biography tour," revisiting key places from his childhood and youth. The tour started in Meridian, Mississippi, where the airfield was named after his grandfather.

Later in the week McCain went to Annapolis and spoke to the midshipmen (including his son and namesake, John S. McCain IV) at the Naval Academy. The idea was to remind voters of his proud military heritage and his own impressive military service. He didn't need to say that neither Senator Clinton nor Senator Obama had served in the military, and they were arguing about which one of them was better fitted to be commander in chief.

During the primary elections, John McCain had striven to appeal to conservative Republicans, the core of the party. But now that he had the nomination, he worked to appeal to Independent voters as well as to Democrats who might vote for a Republican. Many such Democrats had voted for Ronald Reagan in the 1980s.

More sharply than before, McCain presented himself as a very different Republican from George W. Bush. He criticized the Bush administration's neglect of the global climate change problem and presented his own plan for dealing with it. At the same time, he tried to reassure his conservative base. He stated that his first concern in immigration reform would be to "secure the borders"—to immediately put a stop to illegal immigration. He spoke at the annual meeting of the National Rifle Association, trying at least to get off their enemies list.

At the beginning of June, all the Democratic primary results were in, and Barack Obama had the delegates to win the Democratic nomination. Hillary Clinton endorsed Obama, and he was now the presumptive Democratic nominee. Polls showed that most voters had more confidence in McCain's readiness to be commander in chief of the armed forces, because of his military experience, than Obama's. It was also to McCain's advantage that the troop surge in Iraq, which Obama had opposed, now seemed to have greatly reduced the level of violence in Iraq.

Another weakness of Obama's, as a presidential candidate, was in foreign policy. McCain, in contrast, had had years of foreign policy experience in the Senate. In August McCain's advantage in this area was highlighted by an international crisis: Russia invaded the Republic of Georgia, a small country on its border. McCain deeply distrusted the president of Russia, Vladimir Putin, and he thought President Bush had been seriously misguided in trying to befriend him.

But in the minds of Americans, the economy was the biggest concern, more than ever. The home mortgage crisis continued to deepen. During the summer the price of gasoline spiked, rising from three dollars per gallon in February to more than four dollars per gallon in July. John McCain urged drilling for new oil resources in the United States and pointed out to voters that Senator Obama opposed such drilling.

Senator Obama, on the other hand, had the advantage of being literally a fresh face in national politics. By August 2008 he was only forty-seven, while John McCain was seventy-two, and looked it. McCain brushed off comments about his appearance, joking, "I'm older than the hills and have more stitches than Frankenstein."

The McCain team hoped that the fight between Obama and Clinton for the nomination would hinder the Democrats from pulling together during the general election. Many supporters of Hillary Clinton were deeply disappointed that she had lost, and some even threatened to vote for John McCain. But at the Democratic National Convention in August, Senator Clinton endorsed Senator Obama, and that rift seemed to be healed.

Meanwhile, McCain considered his possible choices for a vice presidential running mate. His first choice was his good friend Senator Joseph Lieberman. Although Lieberman was a Democrat, the two were in sync on several important issues, including the problem of climate change and the threat of Vladimir Putin's Russia.

But McCain's advisers were afraid that if he chose a Democrat, the powerful conservatives in the Republican Party would simply walk out of the Republican National Convention. So instead, at the beginning of September, John McCain introduced Sarah Palin, the governor of Alaska, to the Republican convention in Saint Paul, Minnesota, as his vice presidential candidate.

At first Palin seemed like the right choice. She was young, feisty, and upbeat, and she wasn't part of the Washington, DC, establishment. McCain hoped that as the first woman candidate for the Republican vice presidency, she would appeal to women voters. And right after the convention, McCain's numbers did rise in the polls.

But as the presidential race went on, Sarah Palin began to seem more like a mistake. In interviews, she showed that she knew little about foreign policy. While the Republican base loved her, Independents and even many Republicans doubted that she was prepared to be a heartbeat away from the presidency.

To add to McCain's troubles, the financial crisis worsened, and people blamed the George W. Bush administration. McCain tried to explain that he would handle the economy better. But voters naturally associated Republican senator McCain with Republican president Bush, who after all had endorsed him at a televised appearance in the White House Rose Garden.

On September 15 McCain told a rally in Jacksonville, Florida, that "the fundamentals of our economy are strong." He clearly meant this statement to be reassuring. But Obama immediately jumped on the phrase, using it to imply that McCain just wasn't paying attention to the ongoing financial disaster. Only the day before, one of the largest investment banks, Lehman Brothers, had collapsed, and another, Merrill Lynch, was up for sale.

John McCain met Barack Obama three times for debates. After each debate, polls showed that according to viewers, Obama had won.

As November 4, Election Day, drew near, the tone of the campaign grew meaner. At a rally in Minnesota, one woman told McCain, "Obama is an Arab." Taking back the microphone from her, McCain answered, "No, ma'am. He's a decent family man, citizen, that I just happen to have disagreements with on fundamental issues."

John McCain did not convince that woman, or many others who were against Obama more than they were for McCain. But he did make a lasting impression of how to conduct a decent political campaign. He showed that a politician could be honest and gracious, even in the midst of a fierce fight.

And McCain was still fighting fiercely. The day before the election, he campaigned in seven separate cities. On Election Day itself, instead of going to a movie to relax, he made two last campaign stops, in Colorado and New Mexico.

That evening John McCain and his family, along with his campaign staff, waited for the final election results in a private bungalow at the Arizona Biltmore Hotel in Phoenix. Earlier, McCain had warned his family that he was going to lose, and he instructed his brokenhearted daughter Meghan not to cry in public. In the Eastern Time Zone, he had already lost the key states of Ohio and Pennsylvania.

At 11:00 p.m., when the polls on the West Coast closed, John McCain called Barack Obama to concede the election. Afterward, McCain and his family climbed onto a stage on the Arizona Biltmore grounds. The crowd of his bitterly disappointed supporters started to boo Obama.

But McCain held up his hands to stop them. "Senator Obama has achieved a great thing for himself and his country," he said. He noted the historic importance of this election, which had just chosen the first African American president of the United States. And he urged his followers to offer "our next president our goodwill and earnest effort to find ways to come together."

A few weeks later Senator McCain traveled to Iraq. He had already made several trips to that country during the last few years. He wanted to see for himself how the war was being conducted, and how much progress had been made toward developing a truly democratic government. He also wanted to encourage the troops. And he hoped to have Thanksgiving dinner with one certain American serving in Iraq: Marine Lance Corporal James McCain.

John McCain arrived at the marine base in Anbar, Iraq, too late for Thanksgiving, but he was able to share a dinner alone with his son Jimmy. And for that, he was deeply thankful.

Chapter 14

Statesman McCain

Most winners of a presidential election will *say* that they want to work with the opposing political party, for the good of the whole country. But for a president-elect and the defeated opponent to actually start working together is very unusual. And the Republican Party had been soundly defeated in the election of 2008. Besides losing the presidency, they had also lost more seats in the US Senate and House of Representatives to the Democrats. Yet in November 2008, only two weeks after the election, President-Elect Barack Obama invited John McCain to meet with him.

Obama would consult with McCain several more times before his inauguration in January 2009. Obama genuinely wanted the older senator's input about some of the decisions a new president has to make, such as appointments to important jobs. And McCain appreciated Obama's respect for his long experience in foreign affairs, and his close relationship with the armed services.

As McCain told his friend Senator Lindsey Graham, he heartily approved of some of Obama's choices: General James L. Jones as national security adviser, for instance, and Hillary Rodham Clinton as secretary of state. McCain liked Hillary Clinton personally, and he respected her work in the Senate, including that on the Armed Services Committee.

Although Barack Obama and John McCain had fought each other hard, they thought of each other as rivals, not enemies. On a practical level, President-Elect Obama knew how much influence John McCain had in the Senate, and he hoped to get his cooperation. They had some concerns in common, including immigration reform and campaign ethics.

However, their cordial meetings and conversations didn't mean that Senator McCain would stop fighting. He agreed with President Obama that the United States was in serious economic trouble, but he disagreed vigorously with the spending bill the president proposed. McCain and Obama agreed that the United States should get out of Iraq, but not on how.

They agreed that the United States needed better health care, but not on how to provide it.

Before long John McCain was leading the Senate opposition to Obama's policies. One issue in particular would come up over and over again. McCain thought that President Obama was too timid about using US military might—for instance, to settle the war in Afghanistan once and for all.

In 2009, Barack Obama's first year in office, his major project was a health care plan, aiming to provide medical insurance for almost all Americans. His most powerful ally in the Senate was Ted Kennedy, Democrat of Massachusetts, called "the Lion of the Senate" for his political influence. Kennedy had worked hard since the beginning of his long Senate career to achieve health care reform.

McCain, along with most of the Republicans in Congress, fought bitterly against the Patient Protection and Affordable Care Act, or "Obamacare," as it was called. But since the Democrats were in the majority in both the Senate and the House of Representatives, they managed to pass a version of the health care plan without any Republican support in the Senate. President Obama signed the plan into law in March 2010.

John McCain warned that forcing the Affordable Care Act (ACA) through Congress without Republican consent was a big mistake. The Democrats, he said, had "poisoned the well in what they've done and how they've done it." He assured them that they would get no cooperation from the Republicans for the rest of the year.

In spite of being so angry with the Democrats, McCain had sympathized with his friend Senator Ted Kennedy's desire to achieve health care reform. He was sad that Kennedy had not lived to see his victory. In 2008 Senator Kennedy had been diagnosed with malignant brain cancer, and he died in August 2009. At a memorial service, John McCain praised Kennedy's outstanding national service and described fondly their sometimes combative friendship. "Ted and I shared the sentiment that a fight not joined was a fight not enjoyed."

Republicans would continue to attack the ACA for many years, weakening the application of the program. The Republican Party had changed a great deal since the 1980s, when McCain's hero Ronald Reagan was president. In 2009 a movement of mostly conservative Republicans arose, calling itself the "Tea

Party." They believed that taxes were too high, the government spent too much, and the government interfered too much in the lives of citizens. They were reluctant to work with other political groups, and they strongly opposed most of President Obama's agenda.

In 2010 Senator McCain was up for reelection in Arizona. For the first time since 1982, he had a Republican primary challenger, former congressman J. D. Hayworth, who just might beat him for the nomination. Hayworth called himself "the Consistent Conservative" and criticized McCain as a "maverick" who all too often worked with Democrats. McCain immediately declared that he was not a maverick, even though he had proudly called himself just that in the subtitle of his 2003 memoir, *Worth the Fighting For: The Education of an American Maverick*. And of course McCain had indeed tried to work with Democrats, including Senator Ted Kennedy, to reform immigration laws.

Immigration was the main issue of the campaign in Arizona. A new state law, requiring immigrants to carry documents proving that they had legal permission to be in the United States, was widely criticized as harsh, unfair, and perhaps unconstitutional. But McCain defended this immigration law as necessary, because the federal government had not secured the borders. He publicly urged President Obama to send 32,000 troops to the southern border, to protect Arizona from drug trafficking and other criminal activity.

McCain also asked Sarah Palin, his former vice presidential candidate, to help him campaign. Palin, who was loved and respected by the Tea Party, spoke at a rally and assured voters that McCain was a solid conservative Republican favoring strict immigration control. That summer John McCain won the Republican nomination.

In November the voters of Arizona sent McCain back to Washington for his fifth term in the Senate. In that same election, the Democrats lost sixty-three seats in the House of Representatives. President Obama ruefully called the elections a "shellacking" for his party. The Democrats were no longer the majority in the House, and many of the new Republican representatives were allied with the Tea Party movement.

One of John McCain's deepest beliefs was that the United States of America had a special mission to support the development of democracy in other nations. The country did this partly by becoming an ever more free and just society itself. But the United States also had a duty to encourage and assist peoples who were struggling against repressive governments. We needed "to support those people directly wherever and however we can," as he put it later.

McCain recognized such struggles in a movement in the Middle East called "the Arab Spring." At the beginning of 2011, on the northern coast of Africa, the citizens of Tunisia, Egypt, and then Libya rose up against their rulers. McCain applauded these movements, especially the full-scale revolt in Libya, against the brutal dictator Muammar Gadhafi.

McCain visited Libya several times before, during, and after the civil war, and he felt strongly sympathetic toward the Libyan people. He and Joe Lieberman were the first members of Congress to call for the United States to intervene in Libya. Secretary of State Clinton also urged President Obama to use military force to help the Libyan rebels. In March 2011 the French air force led the attack on Gadhafi's air defenses, backed up by the United States and other countries in the North Atlantic Treaty Organization (NATO).

Senator McCain cheered the rebels' victory over Gadhafi that October. But he criticized the Obama administration for not taking the lead of the NATO forces. Worse, he thought the United States and its allies pulled out of Libya too soon, before the new government could be stabilized.

Back in the United States, the campaign for the presidential election of 2012 was underway. John McCain endorsed Mitt Romney, the former governor of Massachusetts, even before he became the Republican nominee, and naturally he supported Romney against President Obama. But McCain was horrified at the amount of money spent on the campaign: a total of $2 billion. Most of that money was spent on attack ads.

Moreover, one-fourth of the $2 billion was contributed by corporations and special interest groups. This kind of political funding had been strictly controlled until a Supreme Court decision of 2010, *Citizens United*. That Supreme Court ruling was a setback for one of McCain's favorite causes, campaign finance reform. He called *Citizens United* "the worst decision of the United States Supreme Court in the twenty-first century." Some years afterward, still angry, he called it "a mistake made by five justices who never ran for any office and were more naive than a cloistered nun about the corrupting effect of unlimited money in politics."

In September 2012, as the presidential campaign in the United States was nearing its end, the American diplomatic compound in Benghazi, Libya, was attacked by an Islamic militant group. Ambassador J. Christopher Stevens and three other Americans were killed. Senator McCain declared on CBS's *Face the Nation* that this disaster was the result of either "a massive cover-up or incompetence." After an investigation, McCain concluded that it was indeed incompetence, and unwillingness to take responsibility. He helped block the nomination of Susan Rice, Obama's ambassador to the UN, for secretary of state, and McCain's friend Senator John Kerry became secretary of state instead.

At the same time that NATO was intervening in Libya, civil war had broken out in Syria, on the eastern coast of the Mediterranean Sea. Again, McCain urged the Obama administration to help the Syrian rebels against President Bashar al-Assad. McCain warned that if the United States didn't support the moderate rebels, the rebellion would be taken over by anti-US Islamic militants. Furthermore, Russia was making moves toward supporting President Assad.

But Barack Obama had been elected on his promise to bring American troops home. After the costly wars in Iraq and Afghanistan, he did not want to entangle the country in yet another war in the Middle East. In 2013 Senator McCain made a trip to Syria himself to encourage the rebels.

In spite of McCain's differences with President Obama over foreign policy, he and Obama developed more friendly relations after Obama was reelected in 2012. The Affordable Care Act, or Obamacare, had become law in 2010, but it still needed to be funded by Congress. While most Republicans in Congress fought to prevent the Affordable Care Act from taking effect, McCain insisted that this was a waste of time. In October 2013 he was one of the few Republican senators to vote for funding the ACA.

In 2012 President Obama had created a program called Deferred Action for Childhood Arrivals (DACA). DACA gave undocumented immigrants who had grown up in the United States a chance to stay, but it was intended only as a temporary solution. John McCain was still eager to reform US immigration policy, and during 2013 he worked with a bipartisan group of senators, called "the Gang of Eight" by the media.

They hammered out an immigration reform bill that they hoped was acceptable to both Democrats and Republicans. The bill passed easily in the Senate. But in the House of Representatives, controlled by conservative Republicans, it was never even brought up for a vote.

McCain did not hesitate to criticize members of his party when he thought they were wrong. In March 2013 he called some far-right members of the Senate "wacko birds" for opposing US intervention in Syria. Conservative radio talk-show hosts, in turn, called McCain a RINO (Republican in Name Only).

The ugly issue of the United States torturing prisoners came up again in 2014. A bipartisan Senate committee released its report on the CIA's use of so-called "enhanced interrogation techniques" from 2001 to 2006. The report concluded that torturing detainees did not produce helpful information, and that it damaged the United States' standing among other countries. This was, of course, what John McCain had maintained for years.

The Obama administration opposed releasing the report to the public, as damaging to national security, and most Republicans in Congress agreed. But

McCain thought it was necessary for Americans to know what their government was doing in their name. "Our enemies act without conscience," he said. "We must not."

At the beginning of 2015, John McCain achieved a long-awaited goal: he became chairman of the powerful Senate Armed Services Committee. He had served on the committee and worked toward this position ever since his arrival in the Senate in 1987.

As President Obama's second term neared its end, an unusually large number of Republicans considered running for president in 2016. During 2015, seventeen major candidates declared themselves. One of the last to enter the race was Donald Trump, a businessman and reality-show host. In his June announcement, Trump made derogatory remarks about Mexican immigrants.

McCain commented that Trump had "fired up the crazies," meaning that Trump was deliberately stirring up unreasonable fear of immigrants. Senator McCain criticized Trump's remarks as "offensive" not only to Hispanic citizens, but to all Americans.

Donald Trump quickly struck back during a town hall rally in Iowa. He retorted that he didn't like McCain because he was a "loser," having lost the 2008 election for president after Trump donated $1 million to his campaign. More shocking, he belittled McCain's ordeal as a prisoner of war.

"He is a war hero because he was captured," said Trump. "I like people who weren't captured." To many people, this remark was more offensive than calling Mexicans "criminals" and "rapists." Most Americans felt deep respect for combat veterans, especially veterans who had suffered during their service.

Trump never apologized to McCain. During the campaign he spoke approvingly of the use of torture to gain information from prisoners. He promised to bring back waterboarding and worse, if he were elected president. McCain later wrote that Trump spoke out of ignorance—not only ignorance about whether torture gets the desired results, but also because he didn't understand that using torture damages our standing with other nations. Most damning of all, McCain said Trump didn't understand that "simple human decency is as essential to the souls of nations as it is to the souls of people."

During the presidential election of 2016, John McCain also ran for a sixth term as senator from

Arizona. If he won, this would probably be his last term, since he turned eighty that summer.

McCain had strong competition from other candidates, both in the Republican primary election and in the general election in November. Feeling pressure not to offend voters, he first said that he would support the Republican candidate for president, whoever was chosen. Then, in March 2016, McCain expressed his doubts that Donald Trump was qualified for the office. Trump struck back, calling McCain "very weak on immigration" and suggesting that McCain might lose his Senate seat because of it. He tweeted that McCain should be defeated in the primaries.

As Donald Trump went from victory to victory in the Republican primary elections, John McCain continued to criticize him: Trump's offensive remarks about women and Muslims, his favorable remarks about the use of torture, and his admiration for Russian president Vladimir Putin. But by early May it was clear that Donald Trump would be the Republican nominee for president. John McCain then finally said he would support Trump, because he was the choice of Republican voters. Trump, in turn, endorsed McCain.

McCain did not attend the Republican convention,

where Donald Trump was cheered as the candidate of the Republican Party. And only a week or so later, when Trump belittled Khizr Khan, a Muslim American whose son, Captain Humayun Khan, had been killed serving in the Iraq War, McCain rebuked Trump sharply. "While our party has bestowed upon him the nomination, it is not accompanied by unfettered license to defame those who are the best among us." In McCain's own campaigning, he said as little as possible about Trump. The Senate race in Arizona against his Democratic rival looked close, and he did not want to miss out on one last term in his beloved US Senate.

By October, John McCain felt fairly certain that he would win his election. At the same time, a video in which Trump boasted about his ability to molest women was made public. McCain announced that he would not vote for Trump *or* for Hillary Clinton. Instead he would write in the name of "some good conservative Republican who is qualified to be president."

On Tuesday, November 8, the voters of Arizona reelected John McCain to the US Senate. And Donald Trump narrowly defeated Hillary Clinton to become president-elect of the United States.

Chapter 15

The Restless Wave

Shortly after the election of November 2016, John McCain took an official trip to Halifax, Nova Scotia, for a yearly conference on national security. One evening a British diplomat, a former ambassador to Russia, offered McCain some information collected by a former British secret agent, Christopher Steele. The informer had told Steele that the Russian government knew some things about President-Elect Donald Trump that could be used to blackmail him.

These allegations were not proven, but they were disturbing enough that McCain thought they should be further investigated. "Even a remote risk that the president of the United States might be vulnerable to Russian extortion had to be investigated," he explained later. So McCain accepted a copy of Steele's report and passed it on to the director of the FBI, James Comey.

Later, when it came out that McCain had given Comey the Steele report, Trump and his supporters bitterly criticized him. But McCain felt that he had only done his duty, as a senator sworn to "defend the Constitution of the United States against all enemies, foreign and domestic." As he put it in his last memoir, *The Restless Wave*, "Anyone who doesn't like it can go to hell."

The Steele report was especially disturbing in light of other signs that Russia might have tried to interfere with the democratic process in the United States. The FBI had been investigating this possibility since July 2016. In January 2017, before Donald Trump was inaugurated as the forty-fifth president, the Senate Armed Forces Committee held hearings on the question of whether the Russian government had tried to influence the election of 2016 with hacking, leaks, and trolling.

John McCain and the other senators on the committee, both Republicans and Democrats, as well as the Office of the Director of National Intelligence, agreed that Russia had tried to prevent Hillary Clinton from being elected. Worse, Russian agents had worked to "undermine public faith in the US democratic process." Their statement contradicted Trump's remarks on Twitter, in which he cast doubt that Russia had interfered.

In May 2017 a special counsel, Robert Mueller, was appointed to investigate Donald Trump's presidential campaign and any Russian interference in the election. Mueller and the investigation were increasingly criticized by the Trump administration and by Republicans in Congress, but the investigation continued well into 2018. John McCain was confident that Mueller, former director of the FBI, would do his duty "diligently, fairly, and nonpolitically."

Even as a candidate, Donald Trump had expressed favorable opinions about Russia and its president, Vladimir Putin. To many Americans, this was surprising—Putin had opposed US interests many times in recent years. In 2013 Putin gave asylum to Edward Snowden, an American official who had leaked classified US information. Russia had made aggressive moves against Eastern European states on its border and had actually annexed the Crimean Peninsula, part of Ukraine. Russia supported the dictator of Syria, Bashar Assad, in the ongoing Syrian civil war.

John McCain had kept a close watch on Vladimir Putin since before 2000, when Putin was first elected president of Russia. On many of his foreign trips for the Senate, McCain had met people in Eastern European countries who felt threatened by Russian aggression. His heart went out to people of any nation who struggled for the rights and liberties guaranteed to Americans. McCain saw Putin as a ruthless, aggressive leader, bent on resurrecting the Russian empire.

McCain agreed with former secretary of state Hillary Clinton that it was useless to try friendliness with Putin, because he would only interpret it as weakness. And Vladimir Putin was a dangerous enemy of democratic governments. "Vladimir Putin is an evil man," McCain stated bluntly. As for Putin, he had put John McCain at the top of a list of "Russia haters" in his English-language propaganda publication, *Russia Today*.

To control Russian aggression, McCain believed, more countries should be included in NATO, the North Atlantic Treaty Organization. NATO had been formed in 1949 to protect the United States, Canada, and Western Europe from the Soviet Union. By 2018, seventeen more countries, mainly from eastern and central Europe, had been admitted to NATO, bringing the membership to twenty-nine.

After Donald Trump's inauguration on January 20, 2017, Republicans were in control of the House, the Senate, and the presidency. At the top of their agenda was doing away with the Affordable Care Act, the health care reform enacted during President Obama's first term. They mounted an intense "repeal and replace" effort. In March the first version failed in the House of Representatives.

In June the House sent a second version of "repeal and replace" to the Senate. John McCain had always thought that there was much wrong with "Obamacare," but he didn't approve of the House bill. He also didn't like the alternative bill the Senate came up with, which McCain called "repeal and good luck to you." And he thought the Republican leaders in the Senate were wrong to try to push through repeal without any Democratic cooperation, just as he thought the Democrats had been wrong to push through the ACA in the first place.

On July 14 McCain had surgery in Phoenix to remove a blood clot over his left eye. The procedure itself was minor, but it turned up some very bad news. He had an aggressive form of brain cancer. It was a glioblastoma, the same deadly cancer that had killed two of his friends: Senator Edward Kennedy in 2009, and Beau Biden, former vice president Joe Biden's son, in 2015.

Many people would have been flattened by this news. John McCain, however, saw it as an opportunity to speak to the Senate about an important subject, one that had been on his mind for some time. On July 25 he returned to the Senate to take part in the ongoing debate about "repeal and replace." McCain walked onto the Senate floor with the surgical wound and stitches clearly visible over his left eyebrow. His fellow senators, Republicans and Democrats, stood up to applaud him.

McCain was deeply touched. He felt still more honored, he said later, that all ninety-nine senators actually stayed and listened to his speech. He spoke of his fierce love for the Senate. He emphasized that the Senate could not function the way it was supposed to unless the members, whatever their party, cooperated. But in these times, both parties seemed more focused on winning than on turning out laws that served the country. "We're getting nothing done," he said bluntly.

Three days later, the Senate's "skinny repeal," the proposed Republican substitute for Obamacare, came up for a vote. Senator McCain had already decided that "skinny repeal" would repeal but not replace the Affordable Care Act—and as a result, millions of

Americans would be left without medical insurance. With the Senate and the media watching, McCain turned his thumb down, casting the deciding vote. Afterward, he claimed that the media made it out to be a much more dramatic gesture than it really was — he'd already informed his colleagues that he would vote against the measure. Still, pictures of McCain in the Senate with his thumb down were splashed all over the TV news, newspapers, and the Internet.

McCain returned to Arizona to begin radiation and chemotherapy treatment. A few weeks later he learned that the USS *John S. McCain*, the navy destroyer named after his father and grandfather, had collided with another ship off the coast of Singapore. It must have been distressing to McCain: the ship whose launching he had so proudly watched in 1994 had been damaged through careless handling. But much worse, the accident had killed ten of the crew.

By then he was feeling the effects of his treatment for cancer. But he didn't hesitate to do what he could: he called each of the families who had lost someone in the accident. He offered his condolences and asked what he could do for them. If they wanted something he could help with, he tried to make it happen.

John McCain returned to his office in Washington

in September. He continued to chair meetings of the Senate Armed Services Committee. He kept working on comprehensive immigration reform. When President Trump decided to end the DACA program, which had given undocumented childhood arrivals a chance to stay in the United States, McCain spoke out. He issued a statement calling Trump's decision "wrong" and "unacceptable."

After December 2017, John McCain was not well enough to travel to Washington, even for votes he thought were crucial. But he kept in close touch with the nation's business, and he kept his hand in by means of phone calls, letters, and Twitter messages.

He continued to criticize President Trump for actions he thought were wrong. In March 2018, when Vladimir Putin was reelected president of Russia, Trump called Putin and congratulated him. McCain tweeted, "An American president does not lead the Free World by congratulating dictators on winning sham elections."

Also in March, President Trump nominated Gina Haspel to be the new director of the Central Intelligence Agency (CIA). During George W. Bush's administration, Haspel had directed a CIA detention center in Thailand. There, prisoners suspected of involvement in the terrorist group Al-Qaeda were subjected to "enhanced interrogation techniques" such as waterboarding.

McCain immediately wrote a letter, addressed to the deputy director of the CIA as well as Haspel, questioning Haspel's nomination. He repeated his conviction that torture was not an effective way to get information from a prisoner, but his main point was about the virtue of his country. "Most importantly, the use of torture compromised our values, stained our national honor, and threatened our historical reputation."

During the Senate confirmation hearings in May, Gina Haspel refused to say that the torture of prisoners conducted under her supervision during George W. Bush's presidency was immoral. Therefore, McCain concluded, she was not qualified to direct the CIA. But he couldn't cast a vote against her confirmation since he was in the hospital at the time. On May 16, 2018, the Senate, including McCain's close friend Lindsey Graham, voted to confirm Haspel. But Democratic senator Dianne Feinstein, who voted against Haspel, called McCain "the conscience of the Senate."

On May 31, Memorial Day, HBO released its documentary *John McCain: For Whom the Bell Tolls*.

The title acknowledged, as McCain himself did, that he was near the end of his life. It was also a tribute to the novel by Ernest Hemingway that McCain had loved since boyhood.

A few days earlier in May, McCain published his new book, *The Restless Wave: Good Times, Just Causes, Great Fights and Other Appreciations*. This title was taken from lines in the "Navy Hymn": "Eternal Father, strong to save, / Whose arm hath bound the restless wave." It expressed John McCain's faith as well as his love of the United States Navy, his first chosen career. The title also referred to McCain's restless nature. As his coauthor, Mark Salter, joked, John McCain could be bound only by the Almighty.

Knowing that *The Restless Wave* would be his last book, McCain used it to warn his readers against the dangers he saw threatening his beloved country. He warned strongly against Vladimir Putin's Russia, bent on weakening the United States and its Western allies and expanding Russian domination. He feared that President Trump's "thoughtless America First ideology," withdrawing the United States from world leadership, meant that other nations without American values — China, Russia — would take our place.

John McCain believed, as he always had, that "the

United States has a special responsibility to champion human rights in all places, for all peoples, and at all times." That sometimes meant military intervention, but most of all it meant speaking up, forcefully, for people who were mistreated by their governments. McCain had done so throughout his career, including for dissidents in South Africa, Syria, Myanmar—and Russia.

Confronting Americans who feared immigrants, McCain stated that the United States had become "the world's freest, most enlightened, and most prosperous civilization" with the help of immigrants from all over the world. He warned that the Trump administration's anti-immigration policies, especially against Hispanics and Muslims, were misguided. Furthermore, they could only hurt the Republican Party.

Although McCain declared himself a "Republican, a Reagan Republican," he warned against the kind of party loyalty that refused to work with the other side. In his campaign for reelection in 2016, his Republican opponent had tried to insult him by calling him a "champion of compromise." McCain commented sarcastically, "Yikes!" *Of course* he compromised with his Democratic colleagues in the Senate, in "principled compromises that move the country forward." That was the way the Senate was supposed to work.

And the Senate, McCain reminded his fellow senators, was meant to be a restraint on the power of the president. In the system of checks and balances that makes up the United States government, there are three *equal* branches: the president and his administration; the federal court system, including the Supreme Court; and Congress—the House of Representatives and the Senate. "Whether or not we are of the same party, we are not the president's subordinates. We are his equal!"

McCain admitted some regrets. One was for his wholehearted support of the invasion of Iraq in 2003. Saddam Hussein, the dictator of Iraq, had not had weapons of mass destruction, as the Bush administration claimed. And so the Iraq War, "with its cost in lives and treasure and security," had been a very serious mistake.

Looking back to the presidential campaign of 2008, McCain was sorry he hadn't chosen Joe Lieberman for his vice-presidential running mate. McCain wasn't blaming Sarah Palin for their loss, he explained, but he'd known "in his gut" that his trusted friend Joe Lieberman was the right choice. The only adviser who'd agreed with him was Lindsey Graham. In retrospect, McCain wished he'd ignored all that good advice and gone with his gut.

Summing up his eighty-one years, McCain wrote how grateful he was for "a happy life lived in imperfect service to a country made of ideals, whose continued success is the hope of the world. . . . I served a purpose greater than my own pleasure or advantage, but I meant to enjoy the experience, and I did."

What was missing from the book was how much John S. McCain's life had meant to other people, both those who knew him personally and those who had never met him. Captain Humayun Khan, the Muslim American serviceman who died in the Iraq War, had been inspired by McCain's books, and so were his grieving parents. President Trump's own secretary of defense, former Marine Corps general James Mattis, said of McCain, "Everything I love about America is resident in this man."

As McCain remained at his ranch near Sedona, Arizona, his seven children visited as often as they could. Longtime friends came to see him: Joe Lieberman, Joe Biden, Lindsey Graham. They sat on the deck with him, watching hummingbirds and hawks, listening to the nearby creek, and hashing over old times and current politics. Former president George W. Bush called to tell McCain that the country was missing him.

Although it was doubtful that John McCain would appear on the Senate floor again, he never resigned. There had been speculation about who might replace him. If McCain either resigned or died before the end of his sixth term, the governor of Arizona would appoint a replacement to serve through 2020. Some believe that the replacement should be his wife, Cindy McCain.

In any case, there will be a new senator from Arizona in the United States Senate. But no one could actually replace John Sidney McCain III: statesman, patriot, friend.

Time Line

August 29, 1936: John Sidney McCain III is born at the Coco Solo Naval Air Station, Panama.

December 7, 1941: Japan bombs the US base at Pearl Harbor, Hawaii.

September 2, 1945: Japan surrenders to the Allied forces, with Vice Admiral John S. McCain Sr. present on the *Missouri*.

September 6, 1945: John S. McCain Sr. dies of a heart attack.

1946–48: Johnny McCain attends St. Stephen's School in Alexandria, VA.

1950: The Korean War begins.

1951: Johnny McCain enters Episcopal High School in Alexandria, VA.

1954: Johnny McCain enters the US Naval Academy at Annapolis, MD.

June 4, 1958: McCain graduates from the Naval Academy.

August 1958: Ensign McCain begins flight training at Pensacola, FL.

October 1962: Cuban Missile Crisis.

November 22, 1963: President John F. Kennedy is assassinated.

1964: Congress gives President Lyndon B. Johnson war powers in Vietnam.

1965: McCain marries Carol Shepp and adopts her two sons.

1966: John and Carol's daughter Sidney Ann McCain is born.

McCain leaves for Vietnam on the *Forrestal*.

1967: In May, John McCain's father appointed commander in chief of the US Naval Forces in Europe.

In July, disastrous fire on the *Forrestal*. McCain transfers to the *Oriskany*.

On October 26, John McCain is shot down over Hanoi and captured.

1967–1973: McCain held as prisoner of war in Hanoi.

April 1968: Dr. Martin Luther King Jr. is assassinated.

June 1968: Senator Robert Kennedy is assassinated.

July 4, 1968: John's father appointed commander in chief of the US forces in the Pacific.

1969: US makes first successful manned moon landing.

September 1969: North Vietnam president Ho Chi Minh dies.

January 1973: The US and North Vietnam sign the Paris Peace Accords.

March 14, 1973: John McCain is released to US custody, leaves Vietnam.

May 1973: President Richard Nixon invites John McCain and other POWs to the White House.

U.S. News & World Report publishes McCain's story of his POW experience.

1973–74: McCain studies at the War College in Washington, DC.

1974: President Nixon is forced to resign due to the Watergate scandal.

1977: The navy assigns McCain to the US Senate liaison office in DC.

February 1980: John and Carol divorce.

May 1980: John McCain marries Cindy Hensley.

November 1980: Ronald Reagan is elected president of the United States.

March 22, 1981: John S. McCain Jr. dies of heart failure.

1982: McCain is elected US Representative for the First Congressional District, Phoenix, AZ.

1984: Meghan McCain is born.

McCain is reelected to the House of Representatives.

1985: McCain returns to Vietnam for a CBS News Special.

1986: John Sidney McCain IV is born.

McCain is elected to the US Senate.

1988: James Hensley McCain is born.

George H. W. Bush is elected US president.

1989: McCain is linked to Keating's Lincoln Savings and Loan scandal.

1990: Saddam Hussein invades Kuwait; the US attacks Iraq.

Cindy McCain brings Bangladeshi baby home to adopt; the McCains name her Bridget.

1992: Bill Clinton is elected US president.

1993: McCain undergoes surgery for melanoma.

McCain helps to monitor free elections in Russia.

1994: Commissioning of the navy destroyer *John S. McCain.*

1995: The United States resumes diplomatic relations with Vietnam.

The McCain-Feingold Act, limiting political contributions, is introduced into the Senate.

1996: President Bill Clinton is reelected.

2000: John McCain runs for president, is defeated in the primaries by George W. Bush. Bush is elected president.

September 11, 2001: Al-Qaeda terrorists attack the US with hijacked planes.

2003: The US invades Iraq.

2004: President George W. Bush is reelected.

2007–2009: The Great Recession.

2008: McCain wins the Republican nomination for president, but Barack Obama wins the general election.

2010: McCain is reelected for his fifth term as senator from Arizona.

The ACA (Obamacare) becomes law.

2012: President Barack Obama is reelected.

2015: McCain becomes chairman of the Senate Armed Services Committee.

2016: Donald Trump, defeating Hillary Clinton, is elected president.

McCain is reelected to the Senate for a sixth term.

May 2017: US Special Counsel Robert Mueller begins investigation of Trump's 2016 campaign and Russian interference in the election.

July 2017: McCain is diagnosed with brain cancer.

McCain flies to Washington, votes down the "repeal and replace" bill.

August 2017: The navy destroyer *John S. McCain* collides with a merchant vessel in the Pacific.

May 2018: McCain publishes *The Restless Wave: Good Times, Just Causes, Great Fights and Other Appreciations.*

August 25, 2018: McCain passes away at his ranch in Cornville, AZ.

Sources

Books

Alexander, Paul. *Man of the People: The Life of John McCain*. New York: John Wiley & Sons, 2003.

Calvert, James. *The Naval Profession*. New York: McGraw-Hill, 1965.

Comey, James. *A Higher Loyalty: Truth, Lies, and Leadership*. New York: Flatiron Books, 2018.

Drew, Elizabeth. *Citizen McCain*. New York: Simon & Schuster, 2002.

McCain, John, with Mark Salter. *Faith of My Fathers*. New York: Random House, 1999.

McCain, John, with Mark Salter. *Worth the Fighting For: A Memoir*. New York: Random House, 2002.

McCain, John, and Mark Salter. *The Restless Wave: Good Times, Just Causes, Great Fights and Other Appreciations*. New York: Simon & Schuster, 2018.

McCain, Meghan. *Dirty Sexy Politics*. New York: Hyperion, 2010.

Povich, Elaine S. *John McCain: American Maverick*. New York: Sterling, 2018.

Timberg, Robert. *John McCain: An American Odyssey*. New York: Touchstone (Simon & Schuster), 1999.

Timberg, Robert. *The Nightingale's Song*. New York: Simon & Schuster, 1995.

Magazines and Newspapers

Bruni, Frank. "John McCain Battles Donald Trump with His Dying Breaths." *New York Times*, May 5, 2018.

Chabot, Hilary. "John McCain: Close Curtain on GOP 'Greek Tragedy.'" *Boston Herald*, February 28, 2012.

Coile, Zachary. "Vets Group Attacks Kerry; McCain Defends Democrat." *San Francisco Chronicle*, August 6, 2004.

Collins, Nancy. "Cindy McCain: Myth vs. Reality." *Harper's Bazaar*, July 2007.

SOURCES

Dickerson, John F. "McCain's Mother: 'Johnny, I'll Wash Your Mouth Out.'" *Time*, February 21, 2000.

Edsall, Thomas B., and Chris Cillizza. "Money's Going to Talk in 2008." *Washington Post*, March 11, 2006.

Eldridge, David. "McCain slams Obama on Libya: 'Nobody Died in Watergate.'" *Washington Times*, October 28, 2012.

Kantor, Jodi. "Vocal on War, Silent on Son's Service." *New York Times*, April 6, 2008.

Kirkpatrick, David D. "After 2000 Run, McCain Learned to Work Levers of Power." *New York Times*, July 21, 2008.

Kirkpatrick, David D. "Obama Reaches Out for McCain's Counsel." *New York Times*, January 19, 2009.

Kranish, Michael. "McCain Brother Stays Out of Spotlight." *Boston Globe*, March 7, 2008.

Leibovich, Mark. "Pedal to the Metal: The Philosophy That Drives Sen. John McCain." *Washington Post*, May 12, 2004.

Leibovich, Mark. "How John McCain Turned His Clichés into Meaning." *New York Times Magazine*, December 22, 2013.

Martin, Jonathan. "At His Ranch, John McCain Shares Memories and Regrets with Friends." *New York Times*, May 5, 2018.

McCain, John. "John McCain, Prisoner of War: A First-Person Account." *U.S. News & World Report*, May 14, 1973.

Mitchell, Alison. "The 2000 Campaign: The Quest; Birth and Death of the 'Straight Talk Express,' from Gamble to Gamble." *New York Times*, March 11, 2000.

Orth, Maureen. "The Road Trip of 2 Lifetimes, and Still Going." *New York Times*, December 14, 2007.

Rutenberg, Jim, et al. "For McCain, Self-Confidence on Ethics Poses Its Own Risk." *New York Times*, February 21, 2008.

Sorkin, Amy Davidson. "The Long Fight." *New Yorker*, May 28, 2018.

Steinhauer, Jennifer. "Confronting Ghosts of 2000 in South Carolina." *New York Times*, October 19, 2007.

Steinhauer, Jennifer. "Bridging 2 Marriages and 4 Decades, a Large, Close-Knit Brood." *New York Times*, December 27, 2007.

Steinhauer, Jennifer. "John McCain Denounces Donald Trump's Comments on Family of Muslim Soldier." *New York Times*, August 1, 2016.

Stolberg, Cheryl Gay. "McCain May Be the Conscience of the Senate. Is Anyone Listening?" *New York Times*, May 10, 2018.

Waxman, Olivia B. "The Moving Way John McCain Honored Sailors Killed on the Ship That Bears His Name." *Time*, May 28, 2018.

Videos
60 Minutes, CBS News, September 24, 2017.

Faith of My Fathers. Dramatization of John McCain's memoir. A&E Television Networks, 2005.

Frontline, PBS, "McCain," Season 36, Episode 8.

"John McCain: American Maverick." *Biography*. A&E Television Networks, 1999.

John McCain: For Whom the Bell Tolls. HBO documentary, 2018.

Vietnam P.O.W.s: Stories of Survival. Discovery Channel documentary, 2000. Includes interviews of McCain and several other POWs from the "Hanoi Hilton."

Internet
ABC News, Nov. 17, 2008. Tapper, Jake. "Obama, McCain Meet While Bill Speaks about Hillary." https://abcnews.go.com/Politics/story?id=6274538&page=1

azcentral, October 15, 2016. "Here's a blow-by-blow account of the Donald Trump vs. John McCain feud," by Dan Nowicki, *Arizona Republic*. https://www.azcentral.com/story/news/politics/azdc/2016/10/15/donald-trump-vs-john-mccain-feud/91960246/

azcentral, July 1, 2018. "Sen. John McCain in physical therapy, former staffer says," by Bree Burkitt, *Arizona Republic*. https://www.azcentral.com/story/news/politics/arizona/2018/07/01/sen-john-mccain-physical-therapy-former-staffer-mark-salter-says/749657002/

The Campaign Finance Institute, a research institute on money in politics in state and federal elections, http://www.cfinst.org

Office of the Clerk of the House of Representatives, Final Vote Results for Roll Call 165, March 21, 2010. http://clerk.house.gov/evs/2010/roll165.xml

SOURCES

CNN Politics, August 3, 2016. "Khizr Khan: John McCain was my son's 'hero'," by Chris Moody. https://www.cnn.com/2016/08/03/politics/khizr-khan-donald -trump-john-mccain/

CNN Politics, December 10, 2014. "McCain makes passionate defense for torture report's release," by Alexandra Jaffe. https://www.cnn.com/2014/12/09 /politics/mccain-lauds-release-terror-report/

CNN Politics, June 17, 2012. "McCain on campaign finance: 'The system is broken'," by Holly Gilbert. http://politicalticker.blogs.cnn.com/2012/06/17/mccain -on-campaign-finance-the-system-is-broken/

Office of the Director of National Intelligence, January 6, 2017. "Assessing Russian Intentions and Activities in Recent Elections." https://www.dni.gov/files /documents/ICA_2017_01.pdf

Gallup, April 11, 2008. "Bush Job Approval at 28%, Lowest of His Administration," by Frank Newport.
http://www.gallup.com/poll/106426/Bush-Job-Approval-28-Lowest- Administration.aspx

Guardian, U.S. edition, October 9, 2016. "John McCain withdraws support from Donald Trump over groping boasts," by Sabrina Siddiqui, Ben Jacobs, and Edward Helmore.
https://www.theguardian.com/us-news/2016/oct/08/john-mccain-donald-trump -sex-boast-tape

Hill, March 22, 2010. "McCain: Don't expect GOP cooperation on legislation for the rest of this year," by Michael O'Brien. http://thehill.com/blogs /blog-briefing-room/news/88285-mccain-dont-expect-gop-cooperation-the-rest -of-this-year

Hill, May 30, 2018. "Arizona governor huddles with John and Cindy McCain," by Scott Wong. http://thehill.com/homenews/senate/389977-arizona -governor-huddles-with-john-and-cindy-mccain

John McCain, U.S. Senator, https://www.mccain.senate.gov/public/

Senator John McCain's official website, August 28, 2009. "Remarks by Senator John McCain at the memorial service for Senator Ted Kennedy." https://www.mccain .senate.gov/public/index.cfm/2009/8/post-70fa80b8-e62c-423e-dac4-1af9740eb68a

KTAR News, May 31, 2018. "Ducey shuts down rumors of Cindy McCain's appointment to the Senate," by KTAR.COM. http://ktar.com/story/2089279 /ducey-shuts-down-rumors-of-cindy-mccains-appointment-to-senate/

SOURCES

The New Yorker, July 16, 2015. "John McCain has a few things to say about Donald Trump," by Ryan Lizza. https://www.newyorker.com/news/news-desk /john-mccain-has-a-few-things-to-say-about-donald-trump?intcid=mod-latest

National Public Radio (NPR) Election 2008, http://www.npr.org/templates /topics/topic.php?topicId=1102#/

New York Times, May 10, 2018. "McCain may be the 'conscience of the Senate.' Is anybody listening?" by Sheryl Gay Stolberg. https://www.nytimes .com/2018/05/10/us/politics/john-mccain-torture-gina-haspel.html

New York Times, November 7, 2012. "Little to Show for Cash Flood by Big Donors," by Nicholas Confessore and Jess Bidgood. https://www.nytimes .com/2012/11/08/us/politics/little-to-show-for-cash-flood-by-big-donors.html? _r=0&pagewanted=all

New York Times, January 5, 2017. "Countering Trump, Bipartisan Voices Strongly Affirm Findings on Russian Hacking," by Matt Flegenheimer and Scott Shane. https://www.nytimes.com/2017/01/05/us/politics/taking-aim-at-trump -leaders-strongly-affirm-findings-on-russian-hacking.html

PBS News Hour, May 22, 2018. "John McCain wants us to see we are more alike than different." https://www.pbs.org/video/maverick-1527024029/

Taegan Goddard's Political Wire, October 15, 2008. "Instant Debate Reaction." https://web.archive.org/web/20081019025913/http://politicalwire .com/archives/2008/10/15/instant_debate_reaction.html

Real Clear Politics, July 19, 2015. "Trump on McCain: 'He is a war hero because he was captured . . . I like people who weren't captured'," by Tim Hains. https:// www.realclearpolitics.com/video/2015/07/19/trump_on_mccain_he_is_a_war _hero_because_he_was_captured_i_like_people_who_werent_captured.html

Reuters, March 23, 2018. "McCain presses Trump CIA nominee over her record on interrogations," by Patricia Zengerle. https://www.reuters.com/article/us-usa -trump-haspel/mccain-presses-trump-cia-nominee-over-her-record-on -interrogations-idUSKBN1GZ2FW

U.S. News & World Report, September 15, 2008. "Seriously? John McCain on the Fundamentally Sound U.S. Economy." https://www.usnews.com /opinion/articles/2008/09/15/seriously-john-mccain-on-the-fundamentally -sound-us-economy

U.S. News & World Report, October 21, 2008. "Data Points: Presidential Campaign Spending." https://www.usnews.com/opinion/articles/2008/10/21 /data-points-presidential-campaign-spending

SOURCES

The Washington Post, March 20, 2018. "Trump congratulates Putin on his reelection, discusses U.S.-Russian 'arms race'," by Jenna Johnson and Anton Troianovski. https://www.washingtonpost.com/world/trump-congratulates-putin-on-his-reelection-kremlin-says/2018/03/20/379effd0-2c57-11e8-8dc9-3b51e028b845_story.html?utm_term=.404862fc52ce

Acknowledgments

I wrote the first version of *John McCain* during the election campaign of 2008. At the same time, I was writing a biography of the Democratic candidate for president, Barack Obama. My agreement with Simon & Schuster was that the winner's story would be published, and so *Barack Obama: Our 44th President* came out at the end of 2008. As for my biography of McCain, I reluctantly filed it in Unpublished Books.

Now I'm delighted to thank everyone who helped bring McCain's story into print, ten years later: My husband, Bob, who urged me to suggest the project; my agent, Susan Cohen, who thought it was a great idea; my editors at Aladdin, Ellen Krieger (for the 2008 version) and Karen Nagel (for 2018); as well as all the editorial and production staff who worked on *John McCain: An American Hero*.

About the Author

Beatrice Gormley has written many books for young readers, including several titles in the Childhood of Famous Americans and Childhood of World Figures series, as well as biographies of Barack Obama, George W. Bush, Laura Bush, Nelson Mandela, and Pope Francis. She lives in Massachusetts.